Markham in Peru

Clements Markham as a young man.

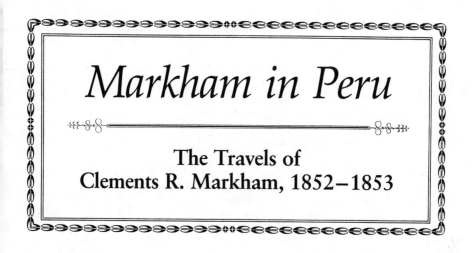

Markham in Peru

The Travels of
Clements R. Markham, 1852–1853

Edited by Peter Blanchard

UNIVERSITY OF TEXAS PRESS, AUSTIN

First Edition, 1991

Requests for permission to reproduce material from
this work should be sent to Permissions, University of
Texas Press, Box 7819, Austin, Texas 78713-7819.

Library of Congress Cataloging-in-Publication Data
Markham, Clements R. (Clements Robert), Sir,
1830–1916.
   Markham in Peru : the travels of Clements R.
Markham, 1852–1853 / edited by Peter
Blanchard. — 1st ed.
      p.   cm.
   Includes bibliographical references and index.
   ISBN 0-292-71132-8 (cloth). —
ISBN 0-292-75127-3 (paper)
   1. Peru—Description and travel.   2. Markham,
Clements R. (Clements Robert), Sir, 1830–1916—
Journeys—Peru.   I. Blanchard, Peter, 1946–
II. Title.
F3423.M33   1990
918.504'5—dc20   90-36144
                                        CIP

Portrait of Markham as a young man (frontispiece)
reproduced by courtesy of the Royal Geographical
Society, London.
Illustrations from Markham's manuscript
reproduced from Wellcome MS American 126,
Wellcome Institute Library, London. By courtesy
of the Trustees of the Wellcome Trust.

Contents

Acknowledgments   *vii*

Map: Clements Markham's Travel in Peru, 1852–1853   *viii*

Introduction   *ix*

1. Pepperell to Lima   *1*

2. Lima   *7*

3. Excursions from Lima   *15*

4. Lima to Cañete   *22*

5. Cañete   *29*

6. Cañete to Pisco   *37*

7. Ica to Nazca   *44*

8. Crossing the Andes   *55*

9. Ayacucho   *61*

10. Excursions from Ayacucho   *69*

11. Ayacucho to Cuzco   *77*

12. Cuzco   *86*

13. The Valley of the Vilcamayo   *100*

14. *Montaña* of Paucartambo   *110*

15. Across the Andes from Cuzco to Arequipa   *116*

Epilogue   *127*

Notes   *133*

Bibliographical Essay   *139*

Index   *145*

Acknowledgments

I WISH to mention several people and institutions that assisted me in completing this book. I must thank first of all Robin Price, deputy librarian and curator of the American Collections of the Wellcome Institute for the History of Medicine in London. Robin brought the Markham manuscript to my attention over eight years ago and has followed its progress with interest, advice, and support. The Wellcome Institute gave me unlimited access to the manuscript, which is deposited in its library, and the trustees of the Wellcome Trust have kindly given me permission to publish the following transcription together with some of Markham's original drawings. I am indebted to Dr. John Hemming and the staff of the Royal Geographical Society in London, especially the chief librarian and the archivist, who dug into their large Markham collection to try to satisfy my many requests. The Royal Geographical Society provided the portrait of Markham. Also in London, the staffs of the Institute of Latin American Studies, the Institute of United States Studies, the Peruvian embassy, the University of London Senate House Library, the Institute of Historical Research, and the British Library helped to clarify points and track down and correct inconsistencies and mistakes in the manuscript. A

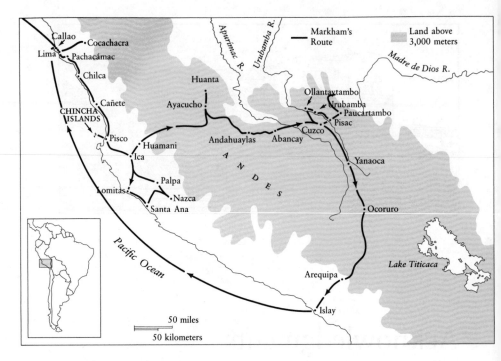

Clements Markham's Travel in Peru, 1852–1853

special thanks is due the director of the Institute of Latin American Studies, Leslie Bethell, who gave me a place to work and a great deal of support during my sabbatical in 1987–88 when most of the research for this book was completed. The staff of the Map Department of the Robarts Library, University of Toronto, helped me to trace Markham's route. The University of Toronto's Cartography Department drew the map included with the text. Small grants from the Social Sciences and Humanities Research Council of Canada financially assisted both my research and the publication of the manuscript.

And, as always, my biggest debts are to Joanna and Adam.

Introduction

IN OCTOBER 1852 a young Englishman named Clements Markham disembarked at the port of Callao, Peru, on the beginning of what was to be a ten-month visit to this South American country. Peru had been the center of the ancient Inca empire, and Markham's goals were to travel to Cuzco, the Inca capital, since, as he noted, no previous English traveler had visited and left a narrative of a trip there, and to assist in "elucidating the former condition of this remarkable country" by examining the actual scene of the deeds of the Incas. His travels would take him to the three major geographical regions that divide Peru from north to south: the narrow coastal strip, a desolate and forbidding desert cut by a small number of verdant river valleys; the majestic Andes, where the Inca empire had been centered and the majority of the Peruvian population continued to live; and the mysterious Amazonian jungle. During his stay he came to know numerous cities, towns, hamlets, and rural estates. He enjoyed the hospitality of Peruvians of all classes and racial backgrounds. He mixed with past, present, and future presidents as well as black slaves and Indian peasants. He noted and commented upon the vestiges of ancient civilizations he chanced to see as well as the flora and fauna he encountered. And as he traveled he recalled some of the principal events in the history of this country that remained a focus of his attention for the rest of his life.

Markham's interest in Peru had been stimulated during a previous visit a few years earlier. Born in 1830 in the village of Stillingfleet in Yorkshire, the son of the Reverend David F. Markham and Frances N. Milner and the great-grandson of a former archbishop of York, he had grown up in an environment of privilege and comfort. Educated at Cheam and Westminster, he had mixed with royalty and nobility from the time of his birth. His father had among his appointments a canonry at Windsor that involved ministering to and meeting socially with the British royal family. In 1844, with his family's approval, Clements joined the Royal Navy as a cadet. His first posting was to the Pacific on board H.M.S. *Collingwood*, whose duties included showing the flag along the western coast of South America and elsewhere in the South Pacific. It was at this time that Markham first visited Peru and came to know its people and their history. Early in 1845 he disembarked at Callao and over the next three years he returned on several occasions as the *Collingwood* carried out its duties. His growing fascination with the ancient homeland of the Incas aroused his desire to explore the country further and to visit Cuzco. In anticipation he began reading all that he could about Peru and its history and learning a bit of Spanish.

At the same time Markham was formulating a second desire that was as firm, as uncertain of accomplishment, and ultimately as vital to his later career as his desire to explore Peru. In response to his experiences aboard the *Collingwood* and despite being promoted to midshipman, he developed a growing aversion to the navy and resolved to resign from the service at the first opportunity. He informed his family of his feelings on his return from the Pacific in 1848. They, however, felt differently, and as they continued to exert a profound influence over his decisions, he remained in the service. Further experience did not alter his views, especially as his next posting on H.M.S. *Superb* involved spending virtually an entire year anchored at Spithead and Cork. At the end of 1849 he resolved once again to leave the service but first had to "muster up courage to speak to my Father about it." The fact that he remained in the navy suggests that he either failed to have the conversation or once again was convinced to remain in harness, at least for a while longer.

Given the opportunity to participate in expeditions he considered interesting, stimulating, and worthwhile, Markham was willing to postpone his departure. This was the case in 1850–51, when he served on board H.M.S. *Assistance* as part of an expedition to the Arctic in search of Sir John Franklin. Despite the diversions and hardships of the expedition, his obsession with Peru remained as strong as ever. While stuck in the ice during the winter of 1850–51 he reread William Hickling Prescott's classic history of the conquest of Peru so that he knew it "almost by heart," and by a stroke of good luck he discovered copies of Quechua grammars on the *Assistance* and began working "indefatigably" on that Andean Indian language. His passion for Peru and the Incas also manifested itself in writing about them. He had written a history of Peru on board the *Collingwood* and now wrote another, as well as a tragedy about the eighteenth-century Peruvian Indian leader José Gabriel Condorcanqui, Túpac Amaru II.

By September 1851, however, Markham had had enough of the navy and was determined to leave. On September 24 he wrote to his parents:

> I dislike the way of life, the kind of study required in the profession, am unsuited for it, and consequently have neither the means nor the wish to attain any eminence in a service which I dislike; and to plod along in it in a station below mediocrity would be misery to me, and also would be wrong. All my wishes, hopes, and aspirations are entirely apart from the Navy, and though, far from looking back on the years spent in it as lost time, yet the day I leave . . . will be one of the most satisfactory of my life.

After successfully completing his gunnery examinations in December he finally achieved his wish.

Markham now began seriously preparing for his trip to Peru, reading other accounts and histories of the country and continuing to study Quechua, although he had not yet informed his parents of his plans. His father had unwillingly agreed to his decision to leave the navy and now wanted Clements to pursue a career in law. Going against his father's wishes was obviously not easy for the younger Markham, and having to reveal his goals in which law played no role seems to have weighed heavily on his mind. His father noted in his diary on June 26, 1852, that Clements "seems very low and unwell. I cannot make him out. All his fine joyous spirits are gone." Finally, five days later, Clements divulged "his anxious wish to go again to South America and search the interior for Peruvian remains." His father opposed the plan, perceptively noting that "his grand object is to obtain materials for history. It is a sad unsettling business this taste for writing, and I fear will turn out most unprofitable." The prospect of losing contact with his son for another year must also have contributed to his opposition. Two years earlier he had watched his elder son die slowly and painfully from tuberculosis, and recently one of his daughters had married. Nevertheless, as Clements noted, "he never refused me anything" and despite his misgivings agreed to the enterprise. He offered £500 toward expenses and assisted in other ways, participating in the purchase of Clements's outfit and writing to acquaintances in order to obtain letters of introduction.

On August 20 the journey began. Markham set out from Windsor, not realizing that he would never see his father again. He proceeded to Liverpool and from there crossed to Halifax on board the *America* with two former messmates from the *Collingwood*. When he shook hands with them at Windsor, Nova Scotia, on September 12 "and really started on my Peruvian expedition, I felt that then I finally left the navy." He added, "I had been very happy in the navy, I had made many friends, yet my resolution was probably a wise one. Still I felt a pang of sorrow and regret." From Windsor he made his way to St. John, New Brunswick, where his account begins.[1]

Markham's principal aim during his travels in Peru was to learn as much as possible about the Incas. He had already developed some theories about their origins and culture that he now intended to test. He planned to do so by visiting, measuring, drawing, and describing as many of the ancient ruins that dotted the Peruvian landscape as possible and by observing the modern descendants of the Incas. He was also fascinated by the sixteenth-century Spanish conquest of the Incas and the legendary exploits of the conquistadores: Francisco Pizarro, Diego de Almagro, and their cohorts. Among the events he mentions in his manuscript are Pizarro's capture of the Inca emperor, Atahualpa, in 1532, Atahualpa's collection of a fabulous ransom in an unsuccessful attempt to buy his release, and the subsequent animosity that developed between Pizarro and Almagro that led to civil war and the deaths of Pizarro, Almagro, and many others. Markham's historical references indicate a particular indebtedness to Prescott's work, but he also read, either before his visit or subsequently, some of the early Spanish chroniclers, whose influence is apparent as well.

The other watershed in Peruvian history that attracted Markham's attention was the revolutionary or independence period. Peru had declared its independence from Spain only thirty-one years earlier, and the events leading to that declaration, the exploits of the great Venezuelan liberator, Simón Bolívar, and the concluding battles of Junín and Ayacucho in 1824 that had decided Peru's fate remained topics of conversation and debate. Many of the participants were still alive and willing to share their memories with an inquisitive young English traveler. Moreover, some of the accounts that Markham read as preparation for his visit focused on this period so that he was as conversant with it as the more romanticized earlier periods of the Incas and the conquistadores.

The Peru that Markham visited in 1852 was a country still dominated to a great extent by its colonial past, although it was now beginning to show some signs of change. The struggle for independence had been long and hard and accomplished only through the intervention of outside forces. Many of the Peruvian elite had remained committed to Spain and Spanish rule and only grudgingly accepted separation from the mother country. They were the major beneficiaries of independence, but they left the running of the new republic in the hands of the military leaders who had made their reputations in the wars. The result was years of political instability as contending military figures competed for control of the country. It was only in the 1840s with the political success of Gen. Ramón Castilla that a degree of stability was finally achieved. As a consequence, an election rather than the usual coup d'état determined the selection of a new president the year before Markham's visit. Nevertheless, the central government had not yet secured complete control and the country was far from pacified. Bands of robbers and highwaymen infested the countryside, attacking travelers and remote farms at will and making travel by an individual dangerous, even foolhardy. Moreover, further political unrest remained a very real possibility as ambitious military men still eyed the presidency. The year following Markham's departure a new civil war erupted, returning Castilla to the presidency and profoundly affecting the lives of many of the people Markham encountered during his visit.

As a result of the years of political turmoil, the country's economy was virtually in ruins. Mining, the key sector of the colonial economy, had been severely disrupted during the independence wars and was still recovering thirty years later. The agricultural sector was weak and backward and the major crops like sugarcane, grapes, cotton, and foodstuffs sold mainly to internal markets. By the 1850s, however, some improvements were evident as a new commodity had emerged to stimulate the economy. In the 1840s Peru began to exploit commercially the vast reserves of bird dung or guano that covered the islands off its coast. In the hands of the British consignees, Antony Gibbs and Sons, sales of this nitrate-rich fertilizer expanded and the extraction and sale of guano soon became Peru's principal industry. Lauded as the panacea for the country's multitudinous economic ills, it provided much-needed revenue and was the impetus behind the modernization that Markham observed as he traveled along the coast. A railway was constructed, more and more rural estates were introducing modern machinery, and coastal agriculture was shifting from the production of foodstuffs to commercial crops. The agrarian sector was finally beginning to expand after years in the doldrums. The number of modernizing estate owners, however, was still small and the impact of their endeavors on the country as a whole remained limited. Although responsive to the new trends, they were still firmly committed to the old ways, to a style of life that the conquistadores had introduced and that their nineteenth-century heirs wanted to see retained.

This was characteristic of the social sphere as a whole. Indians continued to constitute the vast majority of the population, living in the interior highlands and following a style of life that had remained much the same for generations. As descendants of the Incas they were of particular interest to Markham, and he quickly developed strong feelings of affection and sympathy for them. He also sympathized with the black slave population, who resided primarily along the coast, laboring on rural estates and in the urban centers. Slavery was gradually dying out by the early 1850s and slaves were being replaced to some extent by Chinese coolies, who had been imported to work on the guano islands and coastal plantations. The lower class of Peru also comprised a large mixed-blood population, who resided throughout the country and filled a variety of occupations as workers and artisans.

Dominating Peruvian society, as it had since the conquest, was a small white elite who were Markham's main hosts during his travels. They supplied him with the comfortable beds and good meals that from his frequent references seemed to constitute a vital measurement of what he considered acceptable levels of hospitality, even civilized behavior. His own background meant that he had little difficulty relating to or associating with them, although they were the direct heirs of the Spanish "barbarians" who had destroyed the Inca civilization that he admired. Their values and views probably differed little from his, for despite his apparent sympathy for the underdog he was no liberal. He criticized the abrupt way in which Peruvian slavery was abolished two years after his visit, and he wrote shortly after returning from Peru that "the true lovers of liberty have ever fought on the side of loyalty and honour, while republicans and self-styled liberals have proved the greatest enemies of real freedom." Markham found much to admire among the conservative, paternalistic elite, whose economic situation had begun to improve as a result of the guano boom and who made his stay in Peru comparatively comfortable, safe, and enjoyable.

Following his visit in 1852–53 Markham's contacts with Peru tended to be more literary than personal. He made one more visit, in 1860–61. Accompanied by his wife, he headed a British government expedition to obtain cinchona cuttings and seeds from the southern part of the country. The government hoped ultimately to propagate cinchona cultivation in India and develop the production of quinine on a commercial scale in the colony. Markham never returned but he retained his affection for Peru and continued to study its history and pay close attention to its fortunes.

He maintained contact with many of the people he had encountered in his visits, primarily through letters. Among them were two who appear prominently in the following pages: Dr. Francisco de Paula Taforo, a Chilean cleric who accompanied Markham on much of his journey through the Andean highlands, and Victoria Novoa, a twelve-year-old girl who traveled with him from Cuzco back to Lima. Markham's continuing interest in the area manifested itself in numerous publications about the history of Peru and the Incas and in translating and editing several of the Spanish chroniclers' accounts of the conquest of Peru that were published by the Hakluyt Society. As a result of his various endeavors, he became the recognized British expert on Peru and Peruvian history.

At the same time, Markham was establishing his reputation as a prominent figure in geographical circles. He was secretary and then president of the Royal Geographical Society for many years and was involved in a variety of other geographical activities. In his later years, while his Latin American interests did not wane, he became a firm proponent of polar exploration and supported it with the fervor that marked all the passions of his life. He was the prime motivating force behind Capt. Robert Falcon Scott's expedition to the South Pole in 1912, and its tragic denouement caused him intense grief.

Tragic, too, was Markham's own death. One night in January 1916, reading in bed by candlelight, he set the bedclothes alight. Although he was not badly burned in the ensuing fire, the shock and his advanced years combined to kill him.

The account that follows is taken from a manuscript written by Markham entitled "Travels in Peru in 1853." Two volumes in length, it comprises maps, pictures, over 150 drawings by Markham, watercolors, photographs, newspaper clippings, letters, genealogies, even wedding invitations, along with the travel account. The manuscript was written between 1908 and 1912 and edited and amended subsequently until Markham's death. It seems to have been based on an original journal that he kept during his visit but that is now lost. Markham's journals for other years still exist, his biographer refers to the existence of a journal, and among the provisions Markham carried with him on his journey were five notebooks that may have been the journal. Many of the details were added later, but his memory was apparently "marvellous."

Markham's experiences in 1852–53 also served as the basis for a book that he published in 1856 whose abbreviated title is *Cuzco and Lima.* Although inevitably the two works cover much the same ground, *Cuzco and Lima* is far more pedagogical than the travel account. It was written with an eye to introducing the English reader to Peru, its history, its culture, and its future prospects. It also contains several differences in detail that anyone interested in making comparisons might like to investigate. The travel version is a more personal account and is largely restricted to Markham's experiences during his trip. It may have been a volume of the memoirs that he had been writing for several years. The immediate predecessor to this manuscript, a description of his life in the navy after leaving the *Collingwood,* was written in 1898–99 and can be found in the Markham Special Collection in the Royal Geographical Society, London. Alternatively, the travel account may merely have been another in the long list of writings that Markham produced during his lifetime, for writing was another of his obsessions, despite his father's reservations. Markham wrote and rewrote books, manuscripts, papers, and articles endlessly. Many of these were published, but countless other histories and memoirs remain unedited and unpublished.

In order to retain as much of the essence of Markham's writing as possible in the following pages, I have tried to keep my editing of the text to a minimum. I have included only the material that was relevant to his travels, removing details that Markham included in footnotes that were usually of a historical or genealogical nature unrelated to his experiences. From the text I have also cut lists of distances, temperatures, and climatic conditions as well as the letters, newspaper clippings, and other addenda. Where it was appropriate I incorporated Markham's footnotes into the text. In order not to interrupt the flow of the narrative, I have indicated only the more significant changes I have made through the use of brackets. A few explanatory endnotes, again indicated by brackets, have been added to explain those points that seemed particularly esoteric. Without indicating them, I have added a few words and made some changes in punctuation and grammar in order to make the text more comprehensible, corrected Markham's spelling mistakes, provided accents, and updated the spelling of Spanish and Quechua words where it seemed appropriate. Markham's spellings were not necessarily wrong, as Spanish orthography was not standardized until after his visit to Peru, while Quechua spelling has been standardized only in recent years, and even now there are many dissenters. His spellings of place-names in several instances also differed from those used by other authorities. Where there is a discrepancy I have accepted the alternative works, as I came to the conclusion that Markham's spellings were not at all trustworthy.

This was also true of some of Markham's chronological and historical details. Minor errors I have simply corrected. If he had had the opportunity to proofread the text with an eye to publication, he would probably have done the same. The larger historical errors I have indicated with brackets or in the endnotes. The errors show that while Markham was a fine writer and a skilled observer, he had definite shortcomings as a historian. This should not be surprising, for Markham had no historical training nor did he have access to the information that we have today. Among his weaknesses was a propensity to accept anecdotes as fact, especially if they fit his preconceived notions. In the case of the Incas he was prepared to accept legends as truth, relying heavily on the laudatory, but not always accurate, chronicle of Garcilaso de la Vega.

The reader should be aware of this weakness and should treat the following account for what it was: the experiences and impressions of a young man of the Victorian age who was the product of a privileged English background and who had certain set ideas about the places he was visiting and the people he was meeting. The resulting travel account makes a fine story, its descriptions of people, places, personal experiences, and the like are probably accurate, but its evaluations, historical references, and conclusions should be taken with at least a grain of salt; in some cases, with a generous helping.

Markham in Peru

Chapter 1

Pepperell to Lima

THE PARTING with [James] Ashby and [William Henry] Gallows Jones at St. John, New Brunswick, broke the last link of my connection with the navy. It was a great wrench, but no doubt the decision was wise. I never could have endured the steamers with their coaling and filth. Steamers are so unlike the ideal of a man-of-war. I now turned my attention to the land of the Incas. I had prepared myself by a study of Garcilaso de la Vega in the bad translation by Sir Paul Rycaut, of Acosta, of Herrera, of the *Noticias Secretas* of Ulloa, of Skinner's *Peru,* being translations from the *Mercurio Peruano,* of Holguín's Quechua grammar, of General Miller's memoirs, of Robertson and Prescott.[1] I had also read the modern books of travel, Tschudi, Stevenson, Proctor, Dr. A. Smith, Scarlett, etc., but they are all more or less rubbish.[2] My age was twenty-two years and two months. I could make a traverse survey and observe for latitude and longitude. My first object was to make the acquaintance of Mr. [William Hickling] Prescott, the historian of the conquest of Peru, for whom I had letters of introduction.

I went from St. John, New Brunswick, to Eastport, in the state of Maine, in a wretched steamer where the Maine liquor law was in force but where spirits could be obtained if called sarsaparilla; thence by train to Boston, putting up at the Revere House, and sending the letters of introduction to Mr. Prescott. I soon received the following welcome:

> Pepperell,
> Sept. 11th, 1852.

My dear sir,

I have had the pleasure of receiving your card this evening (on which, however, you have not mentioned the hotel at which you are staying) together with the notes of my friends, Lord Carlisle and Dean Milman. I regret very much that I am not in town on your arrival. But we are passing some weeks of the autumn at an old farm about forty miles from Boston—where, if you have no objection to "roughing it in the bush," we shall be happy to see you. I should mention that the trains leave Boston for Pepperell at four o'clock in the afternoon, from the Fitchburg *dépot*—what in your land is called a "station." My carriage will be at the Pepperell station on the arrival of the train, at six P.M., on Monday, and if you cannot come on that day, on any other which may be more convenient. I am only sorry that I can offer you no better inducements than a cordial welcome in a quiet New England farmhouse.

> I remain my dear Sir
> Very Sincerely Yours
> Wm. H. Prescott.

I was met at the station by Mr. Prescott and his son, Amory, who drove me to their house, a long wooden building with tall shady trees in front, on a lawn dividing the house from the quiet country road. Our party consisted of Mr. and Mrs. Prescott; Amory; Mr. [John Foster] Kirk, the secretary; and myself. Mr. Prescott was not quite blind; he could see enough to go about the house and to take a walk, but not to read. I passed much time in his large study. The secretary read his authorities to him while he took notes on a slate with lines. The notes were then read over to him, and after some thought he began to dictate. His conversation was most interesting. As regards Peru he explained most lucidly how the authorities I had not seen differed from those I knew and to what extent they supplement each other. These were Zarate, Gómara, Cieza de León, Montesinos, Fernández, Ondegardo, and Pedro Pizarro.[3] Prescott had given closer attention to the proceedings of the Spanish conquerors than to the history of the natives, though his review of Inca civilization is masterly. One day he said that no history could be perfect unless the author was personally acquainted with the localities he had to describe.

Amory Prescott drove me about the state of New Hampshire in a buggy, and we also had a boat in which we pulled on the pretty little river Nissitisset. Some evenings four of us played at whist, but we had to put our hands under the table when the servant brought in the tea as he did not approve of cards. I passed a very interesting and delightful ten days at Pepperell and was very sorry to take leave of my hospitable friends.

From Pepperell I went, by Worcester Junction in Connecticut, to New York, putting up at a humble hotel called Judson's near the Battery. I thought New York an odious place and was glad to leave it after a few days in the *Sierra Nevada* steamer bound for Colón on the eastern side of the isthmus of Panama.

It was the time of the rush after the discovery of the gold in California and an immense number of passengers was going out in the *Sierra Nevada,* loafers and adventurers of all kinds, men with large families, many women by themselves, an extraordinary conglomeration of people. The nicest were some tall youths from Virginia, in broad-brimmed straw hats and red shirts.

Crossing the Isthmus of Panama was a strange experience in 1852 with the railroad unfinished. We landed at Colón on the 2d of October. It then consisted of forty or fifty wooden houses, put up at little expense, in the midst of dense tropical vegetation, springing out of a swamp. Here the Atlantic terminus was established, between Portobelo on one side and Chagres on the other.

I rested in the verandah of the house of the railway superintendent, Mr. Center, while the motley crowd of passengers hurried to the train. At length all was ready, the train started, and away we went deeper and deeper into the dense pestilential forests. At noon the terminus was reached at a place called Barbacoas, the railroad being only finished for a distance of twenty-five miles. The rest of the journey had to be made in boats up the Chagres River and then by mules over the forest-covered water parting. Here the busy crowd of men, women, and children and all the luggage had to be divided among several flat-bottomed boats with wooden awnings. I made up a party of nine men, three women, and seven children for our boat.

The river is bounded on either side by thickly matted tropical forest. The current runs with great rapidity and the boatmen punt with long poles by walking along a ledge round the sides of the boat. The heat was intense and I tried to keep one little boy cool by dipping a handkerchief in the water and putting it round his head. But he kept moaning, "I tant det tool! I tant det tool!" Having stemmed the current for six miles, we reached the miserable village of Gorgona, where we had to remain until the morning, as it is too dangerous to face the rapids in the night. Gorgona consists of a few huts with high conical palm leaf roofs and two so-called hotels. The night passed off slowly and wearily, there being no mosquito curtains for the beds. At length the early dawn appeared and with it a dense mist rising from the teeming forest. Again we started, moving slowly, for the current increased in force at every mile. It was a long eight miles, taking seven hours, but at length we arrived at Cruces, where the river portion of the journey ends. Cruces consists of about one hundred huts ranged along a dirty street, crowded with mules and steaming from liquid filth. The "hotel" was a long hut with a mud floor and a narrow deal table.

The distance from Cruces to Panama is twenty-eight miles through dense forest. There were several "transportation companies" which gave the traveller a receipt and professed to convey his luggage safely to Panama, but the delays in delivery were serious. Their difficulties, owing to the unspeakably bad roads, were great. The chief companies were Taber and Perkins, Hurtado y Hermanos, Agustín Pérez, Henríquez and Woolsey, and José Secundo. I patronized Hurtado because he was a native of position, preferring him to the Yankee speculators, and I was right. The road was probably the most execrable in the world, sometimes leading through swamps of black mud, then up rocky slopes or along torrent beds, then over attempts at "corduroy" roads with the sleepers out of position. I pitied the poor mules. During the whole day parties continued to leave Cruces and brave the horrors of this road. Halfway, in the very depths of the forest, was a long hut with the sign of the elephant, where the charge was two dollars for a cup of tea. After leaving this halting place we were overtaken by heavy showers, the rain coming down in buckets, clothes being converted into a soaking sponge, and so we went on—heavily, despondently. At length, after dark, we reached another long hut consisting of a bar, an eating place, and a sleeping place. Here about forty drenched mortals were congregated and had to pass the night. In the sleeping place were three tiers of bunks and a row of hammocks. There was much confusion, noisy quarrels, and several revolver shots. My companions were Yankees with long tangled hair and beards, eyes bloodshot, sunken haggard cheeks, and hatchet faces, in filthy shirts once red, bowie knives and revolvers—products of the great republic. Day at length dawned after a second night of isthmian horrors. We again mounted our jaded mules and started. Gradually what had been the rocky bed of a mountain torrent became a bridle path, and fields of Indian corn alternating with pastures made their appearance in place of the dense forest. Then the bridle path became a road and the dear old Pacific burst upon our view. We passed through a suburb and under the old gateway and entered the city of Panama.[4]

Panama is bounded on three sides by the sea and is surrounded by a wall and ditch, with two bastions on the land side. In the centre is the

"Modern Yankee vulgarity is everywhere, in flaring advertisements and sign posts of all colours."

plaza with the old cathedral on one side and the municipal building on the other, while through the town runs the Calle de las Monjas [Street of the Nuns]. The old-fashioned Spanish houses, with broad verandahs and folding doors instead of windows, looked sedate and sleepy enough a few years ago, but a revolting change has come over the old town. Modern Yankee vulgarity is everywhere, in flaring advertisements and sign posts of all colours. Painted all over the ground floors are notices in huge letters that "good lodging," "brandy smashes," "egg nogg," "cheap board," etc. are to be had. There were eight so-called hotels for Californian emigrants, all covering their houses with sign boards of all colours and dimensions.

The passengers continued to arrive during the two following days, and on the 8th of October a steamer, the *Golden Gate*, started for California with the majority of them. The rest, whose baggage had not arrived in time, went later in the *Winfield Scott* and Panama became more quiet.

Mr. [William] Perry, the English consul, was extremely hospitable. He has built himself a very handsome stone house looking out over the bay, on the other side of which the towers of old Panama rise out of the dense forest. Mr. Perry is a son of the editor of the *Morning Chronicle*, well known in his day, and brother of Sir Erskine Perry, an Indian judge. He had a very beautiful daughter, married to young Hurtado, and a son, Gerald Raoul Perry, my old messmate in the *Superb*. Their mother was a De Courcy, sister of Lord Kinsale.

In the morning of Saturday, October 9, after six days at Panama, I went

on board the steamer *Quito* and steamed down to the beautiful island of
Taboga, where we found H.M.S. *Daedalus* commanded by Captain
[George Greville] Wellesley. Poor Mr. [William Pitt] Adams, the British
minister at Lima, had recently died, and Captain Wellesley had brought
his widow and her sister, Miss [Elizabeth] Lukin, to Panama on their way
home. He afterwards married Miss Lukin.

On Thursday, October 13, we arrived at Paita, the first stopping place
on the coast of Peru, and took on board the minister of war, His Excellency General Don Crisóstomo Torrico. He sat next [to] me at dinner and
talked intelligently and with knowledge of the campaigns of Condé,
Marlborough, and Wellington.

Next morning we were off the island of Lobos Afuera. A company had
been formed at New York to take the guano off it in defiance of the rights
of Peru. We found the whole Peruvian navy assembled at anchor, with the
bicolour flag flying all over the place. The island was a long range of
white rocks rising about one hundred feet above the sea. The fleet under
Captain Don Domingo Valle Riestra, the commander-in-chief afloat,
consisted of the *Rimac*, a steam corvette with two sixty-eight pounders
and four twenty-four pounders (Commander Don Diego de la Haza); the
Mercedes, an old merchant ship with guns; the *Gamarra*, a gun brig with
sixteen eighteen pounders (Commander Don José Silva Rodríguez); and
two armed schooners, one, the *Libertad*, with one nine pounder (Don
Tomás Ríos). About three hundred soldiers had been landed. So the Yankee pirates did not come, though twenty-three vessels were on their way.

On Saturday, October 16, we arrived at Callao and at nine A.M. I
landed in Peru once more, with all my reminiscences of the dear old *Collingwood* days crowding in my brain. Since those days the railroad from
Callao to Lima, projected and completed by native capitalists, [José Vi-
cente] Oyague and [Pedro de] Candamo, had made the journey easier.
Formerly we went by an omnibus along the very dusty road.

I went to Morin's Hotel in the great square facing the cathedral where I
had often been before when I was a midshipman. Madame Morin was a
sister of my old friend Madame Zuderell at Callao in the *Collingwood*
days. The hotel dining room looked out on the square. Then there was a
passage open to the sky, with doors on either side, each opening on a
good-sized sitting room and a bedroom beyond, both lighted from above.
At the end of the passage was another pleasant room where we often had
dessert. The billiard room was downstairs. There were excellent Chinese
waiters.

It was a great joy to be in pleasant festive Lima once more and its al-
lurements detained me longer than I intended, October 16 to December 8,
fifty-three days.

Chapter 2

Lima

LIMA WAS little changed since I saw it last in 1847. There was, however, one characteristic missing, and that was the ladies in the streets and churches in the *saya y manto* dress.[1] It has gone out of fashion and is rarely seen on fiestas, never worn by fashionable people. Many, however, appear on bullfight days.

My letter of credit was to Messrs. Allsop for £300. Among English residents I also knew Mr. [Samuel] Went, head of the House of Gibbs, and old Reid, a friend of former days. Mr. Pfeiffer, a wealthy German, his wife, and good-looking son and daughter were very friendly and I often dined or spent the evening with them. Young Pfeiffer sang beautifully. I also knew a Mr. Gilbert Brandon, who had married a Peruvian lady, daughter of Dr. Rospigliosi, a judge at Tacna, and with a brother in the army, well informed and with some poetical talent.

Messrs. Murrieta had given me letters to Don Felipe Barreda and Don M. M. Cotes, my best and most hospitable friends. Mrs. Ormsby Gore (afterwards Lady Harlech, a daughter of Sir George Seymour) introduced me to the Codecidos, and Mr. Moore Brabazon (an old Windsor friend) to the Riva Agüeros, a historical family whose grandfather had been the first president. Dr. and Mrs. [John] Gallagher were friends of the *Colling-wood* days, and the chaplain, Mr. [John G.] Pearson, came to make my acquaintance.

Don Manuel M. Cotes was a stout little man, married to the fair Grimanesa Althaus, as charming as she was beautiful. Her grandfather was distinguished in the war of independence, mentioned in General Miller's memoirs, and her brother, Clemente Althaus, was a poet of considerable merit. She was a cousin of the president's wife.

On the 23d of October I received an invitation to dinner at the Cotes, *tomar la sopa,* as they called it. It was a very grand affair with a great display of plate. There were also rows of the large white datura flower, which they call *floripondio,* fixed in light gilt wire frames and filled with smaller flowers. The general effect was brilliant. Among the guests were the venerable Don Pío Tristán, the last viceroy though only for ten days; Dr. [Agustín Guillermo] Charún, the new bishop of Trujillo; Don Manuel Tirado, the minister of foreign affairs; General Torrico, the war minister; Señor Oyague, the financier; Admiral [Francisco] Forcellado; Clemente Althaus, the poet; the ministers from Venezuela and Ecuador; and myself, besides eight others. It was a very interesting dinner and others came in the evening.

On another evening I dined very quietly with the Cotes family to meet the president, General [José Rufino] Echenique, and his wife. He had very good-naturedly brought with him some golden ornaments of the Inca period, recently arrived from Cuzco. One was a breastplate worn by the Inca, a large disc of thin gold representing the sun, and round it what I believe to be signs of the twelve months with the intercalary days. It was very thin, being convex on one side and concave on the other, and the figures upon it were stamped. There were four holes on the small diameter through which a small chain was passed to secure it to the dress.

The second was supposed to be the head of an ornamental pin or *topu* worn by the *coya* or wife of the Inca. It was of thin gold, and the figures on it were cut or scratched and not stamped as in the breastplate. The surface was flat. It is very remarkable that the great majority of figures on this ornament represented most perfect Maltese crosses.

The third was a flat piece of gold with a long stalk and was probably one of the leaves out of the golden garden of the Incas. It was also very thin.

The fourth were four circular pieces of gold, deeply concave, with holes in the centre of each. Two of these ornaments were of exactly the same size made to fit one on the other, and it is probable that the two others also had their fellows which have been retained or stolen by the discoverers. They were probably intended to represent the fruit of the golden garden and once had long stalks, like the leaf, attached to them by the central hole.

The fifth was a long piece of gold, very thin and easily bent, probably used as an ornament to adorn the head (or waist, which must have been very small) of the *coya*.

The figures on the breastplate and pin head were very neatly executed and the circumferences of the breastplate and the fruit were drawn with a degree of mathematical precision which goes far to prove the knowledge of the ancient Peruvians of the principles of the circle and other figures. The leaf was also accurately shaped; and the whole of these most interesting remains lends their aid to prove the high state of the civilization reached by the Incas previous to the devastation of their land by the barbarous and savage Spaniards.

The Peruvians called gold "the tears which are shed by the sun" and extracted it from mines and the *lavaderos* or washings of rivers, finding sometimes lumps of thirty-five to forty ounces and even more. Their most abundant mines were those of Collahuaya, whence the Spaniards also gathered rich fruits.[2] Those barbarians broke up all the golden ornaments and utensils they could find and sent them in bar to Spain so that most of the most perfect have been destroyed, but every now and then some few are discovered in tombs or dug up among ruins. The golden garden in the palace of the Incas is described by every Spanish authority and I think, beyond a doubt, that the above are the fruit and a leaf from that garden. They are by far the most important Inca relics I have ever seen, either in museums or elsewhere.

The president, General Echenique, whose name is Basque, was a prisoner to the Spaniards on an island in Lake Titicaca during the greater part of the war of independence. He is famous as the author of the "Brazo de Maquinhuayo" when, during a civil war [in 1834], he induced the two armies to fraternize and embrace each other. But for the most part he kept out of the civil strifes, living quietly on his estates. He, however, took office under the late president, General Don Ramón Castilla, through whose influence he became president in 1851. I thought him dull but amiable. It is said that Castilla is now extremely dissatisfied with the financial proceedings of the Echenique government.

I improved my acquaintance with Don Manuel Tirado, and he caused a very interesting report on the navigation of the Peruvian tributaries of the Amazons to be prepared for me at the foreign office.

The most cordial and hospitable of my Lima friends was Don Felipe Barreda. He lent me a horse and the groom came every morning for orders, but I only rode it to Miraflores or Magdalena or the alamedas [promenades], not for expeditions. He also gave me the use of his box at the opera; and I often dined and went to *tertulias* or evening parties at his house. His wife was a stately but hospitable lady of the Osma family, daughter of the first Peruvian minister at Madrid. The eldest daughter and the second, who was exceedingly pretty, used to go to the opera with us. I met there a Miss Espantosa, whom I considered to be the prettiest girl in Lima, and I used to visit her in her box at the opera; also three very charming Miss Eléspurus. There were several particularly nice Barreda children, of whom I saw a good deal. I met the former president, General Don Ramón Castilla, at the Barredas with his dignified old wife, of the Canseco family of Arequipa. The Barreda house is all on the upper floor and splendidly furnished, with a white marble staircase. There are three spacious drawing rooms, dining room, library, and smoking room.

I used often to go to the Codecidos, wealthy people, the señora being a sister of the financier Oyague; and there were two charming daughters, one married to [Andrés] Bello, the Chilean writer on international law. Here I used to meet Don Juan Aliaga, the count of Lurigancho, and we became great friends. His house is near the Rimac bridge. I was also welcome at the house of the Riva Agüeros and particularly liked the young son.

Mr. Brandon introduced me to his wife's family, the Rospigliosis, where I sometimes dined and passed the evening. One night a young lady named Villanueva was there, a fresh rosy girl, rather fat, daughter of a very rich farmer who made his money in alfalfa or lucerne, so she was called "La Señorita Alfalfina" or Little Miss Clover. We were sitting talking when there was a violent shock of earthquake. Miss Clover plunged shrieking into my arms. I clasped her to my breast and dashed with all my force at the glass door, bursting it open and smashing all the panes to pieces. In another second we were all huddled together in the middle of the street, Miss Clover still screaming. We waited for the second shock, which was slight, so we went back. "How the earth's tremor has broken the glass!" said the old judge. "No wonder!" replied I.

I also met a very intelligent Peruvian at the Rospigliosis named Don Modesto Basadre who was educated at Downside College near Bath, afterwards studying at London and Edinburgh universities. He writes a great deal in the Lima newspapers and has published some clever essays on Peruvian subjects. Don Modesto told me some stories about hidden treasure. He said that eleven thousand llama loads of gold, part of the Atahualpa ransom, were buried by the drivers on hearing of the Inca's murder. About 130 years ago there lived an Indian woman in the province of Lampa who kept a shop and had a licence to sell spirits. One day an Indian charcoal burner came who wanted to buy something and, not having sufficient money, he gave as a pledge some figures of gold and silver, with a strict charge that the woman should show them to no one. Some time passed and she got short of money. Breaking her word, she took the pledges to a priest, a Dominican named Padre Catalán, asking him to value them, to which he readily agreed. A few days afterwards the owner came with money to redeem the figures. The woman immediately went to the priest for them. Suspecting that they came from some *huaca* [Indian shrine], he insisted on her telling him who the real owner was. After some remonstrance she did so. He was arrested, thrown into prison, and examined as to the place whence he had taken the valuable figures. He indicated a place, where excavations were made, quite fruitlessly. He was then tortured. At length an old Indian came and informed the authorities that it was no use torturing the poor charcoal burner, as he was ignorant; but he explained the locality of a *huaca* where the treasures of some temples were buried, a spacious pond being formed over the excavation. The Dominican, joining with him Don Pedro Aranibar of Arequipa, collected funds and began to work. They soon found gold and silver ornaments to the value of $2,500,000. The place is called Manamchiri in the province of Lampa. Now it is a small lake with an island *huaca* in the centre.

Don Modesto added that it was probable that there are similar deposits in the suburbs of the city of Cuzco, some of which were taken by [Mateo García] Pumacahua when he attempted to throw off the yoke of Spain. He asked an Indian friend's advice how to obtain funds to carry on the war. "I know," said his friend, "of a secret place formed by my ancestors, where there are riches which are to be used when the country is fighting for liberty. This night you shall come with me and take what you require." They entered by a secret opening in a rock, with a light, and came into a chamber full of gold. Pumacahua returned to Cuzco with some of the treasure along the course of the Huatanay [River]. Afterwards he was taken prisoner and hanged at Umachiri.[3] This was in 1814. Pumacahua with his friends, [Domingo Luis] Astete and Angulo, secreted much of the treasure thus obtained on the approach of the Spanish General [Juan] Ramírez, but the locality is unknown. We sat until late in the Rospigliosi verandah, talking over the mysteries of the hidden treasure with Don Modesto Basadre, whose mind was steeped in the folklore of the land of the Incas.

On Saturday, the 13th of November, there was a grand ball given by the marquesa de Torre Tagle, who has the best house in Lima, in the street leading east from the plaza.[4] I was invited and went with the Barredas after dining with them. Every beam in the house is elaborately carved and came out from Spain. We entered into a court by a fine archway and up a splendid staircase to a spacious gallery. The roof was finely carved and supported by light pillars in the Moorish style. The grand reception room where we danced was lined with old cabinets inlaid with silver and mother of pearl. Portraits of ancestors hung round the other rooms, with names and dates duly inscribed on scrolls. There had been four generations of the marquises of Torre Tagle. The last took a leading part in the revolution, but ended by going over to the Spaniards and died in Callao Castle during the siege [1824 to 1826]. The present heiress is married to a lawyer named Sevallos.

Among the guests were the president and nearly all the ministers, old Castilla with his stately dame, General [Antonio Gutiérrez de] La Fuente and his three rather passé daughters, beauties of four years ago, Cotes and the lovely Grimanesa, the Barredas, Codecidos, Riva Agüeros, Espantosas, Eléspurus, Aliagas, all friends of mine, but no English besides myself. It was a brilliant festive scene and very enjoyable. I was not in bed until six A.M.

On the next day there was a grand bullfight in honour of the president's birthday at three P.M. I went to the Aliagas' box. After three or four bulls there was a remarkable event. Gaspar Díaz, the matador, came swaggering in with his sword but missed his aim. The bull ripped his thigh open and was with difficulty drawn off by the picadores. Gaspar was carried out insensible. The performance continued. At last there was a more than ordinarily ferocious bull which was goaded to fury. Then there was a thrill through the great assembly as Gaspar entered on a crutch, pale as death, with his leg bandaged, a sword in his right hand. The bull rushed furiously upon him as he leant upon his crutch. Gaspar plunged the sword in, up to the hilt. He fell on one side, the bull fell dead on the other. The applause was deafening, the excitement intense. One point of interest in the day's proceedings was the appearance of a number of ladies in the alameda dressed in the *saya y manto*, none who was in society but persons of the middle class.

I never once dined at the hotel while I was at Lima, but with all this dissipation I did not neglect the business on which I was engaged. I bought the *Antigüedades Peruanas* of [Mariano Eduardo de] Rivero and von Tschudi which was just out and studied it carefully; also the genealogical work of Dr. Don Justo Sahuaraura Inca, and the Quechua grammar and dictionary of Torres Rubio, from which I filled a notebook with useful words and sentences.[5] I was also much at the museum and library, examining and trying to sketch some of the portraits of the Spanish viceroys and making extracts from some of the interesting volumes of "Papeles Varios."

With regard to my route, I considered that there were three distinct areas of investigation in Peru: that of Chinchasuyu and the civilization to the north, that of the Incas in the centre, and that of the so-called Aymaras to the south. As I had only a year I resolved to devote myself exclusively to Cuzco and the Incas. My journey was to include an examination of the Incarial part of the coast from Lima to Nazca, the crossing of the Andes in two places, the journey to Cuzco, researches at Cuzco and

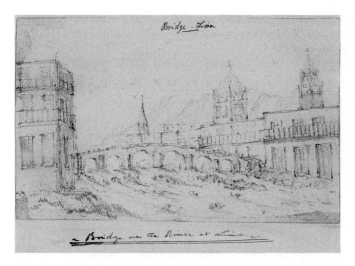

Bridge over the Rimac at Lima

" . . . there was no more festive and hospitable city in the world."

its neighbourhood, an excursion into the *montaña* [jungle], and a return by Arequipa.

This having been settled, the letters were prepared. The president wrote to the prefects of departments I should pass through. I was to go first to Cañete, where I was to be received by the brother of the Señora Barreda, Don Mariano Osma. Other *hacendados* further down the coast were written to, including Don Domingo Elías at Pisco. General Torrico and Cotes wrote to their great friend, General Don Manuel de la Guarda, prefect of Cuzco.[6]

The market for mules was over the bridge on the other side of the Rimac. Several hundreds had just arrived from Tucumán [in Argentina]. Old Mr. Pfeiffer had got me one on trial, but it had so many unpleasant tricks that I declined the animal after it had made rather an exhibition of me in the alameda. So I went to choose for myself. There were two I liked the look of, a black and [a] chestnut. They seemed to be strong and to be fairly good-tempered. The man wanted $150 but I succeeded in beating him down to $90.[7] The chestnut was a mare (*hembra*) with [a brand] on the right haunch. I named her the Cotham after the estate of my ancestors in Nottinghamshire. The black was a male (*macho*) with [a brand] on the left haunch. I named him the Bdellium, being the motto of the Colley Head Society.[8] I kept them in a small corral over the bridge and had several rides up the right bank of the river on them. I then, with the help of Don Modesto Basadre, bought all the necessary mule trappings. I dispensed with a tent and with an *almofrej* [traveling canvas], containing mattress and bedclothes, from motives of economy. They would have required two more mules.

The last three days were fully occupied in taking leave of my numerous friends, and I left Lima with the conviction that there was no more festive and hospitable city in the world.⁹

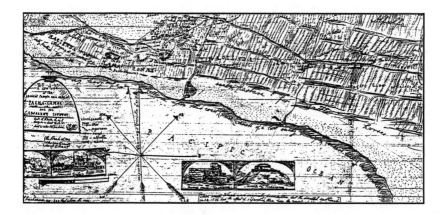

Chapter 3

Excursions from Lima

ABOUT TEN days after I arrived at Lima, a wild young Irishman named Hartrick came to Morin's Hotel from the interior. He told me that he came out to make his fortune and was secretary to Mr. Adams, Her Majesty's minister, for four months. Next he joined General [Juan José] Flores in his expedition to Ecuador [in 1852] and was made his aide-de-camp, but the adventure failed. Hartrick escaped into Peru, reaching Lima penniless. Unable to pay his passage home, he has been obliged to take a situation at Dr. Maclean's silver mine of Tuctucocha, on the road to Tarma, but at a great elevation. There he has to live on llama flesh above the line of perpetual snow, looking after the miners. Once a month he comes down to Lima to take up money to pay them—$2,000.

Hartrick asked me to accompany him as far as the foot of the mountains and help him to defend his treasure if attacked, as the road is infested by a band of mounted robbers—runaway slaves. I readily consented. I did not take Barreda's horse but hired one and armed myself to the teeth with a brace of pistols in my belt, a revolver in my trouser pocket, a long knife down one boot, and a life preserver down the other.

This made me look so like a brigand myself that I put on a poncho over all. I was on a grey horse, Hartrick on a mule with the $2,000.

We started early in the morning of October 29. The first stage was about eighteen miles through the fertile valley of the Rimac, running northeast from Lima, to the little village of Chaclacayo. The river here becomes a torrent and is bordered by canes averaging twenty feet in height and growing so closely as to be almost impenetrable in many places. Large willow trees line the road, with here and there the white bell-shaped flower of the datura. Small hawks, pigeon, and ground doves abound, and turkey buzzards soar among the rocky peaks. There is a large black pie called [*tijereta*] because its tail is like a pair of scissors and many brightly coloured finches. Herds of oxen were grazing in the lucerne fields. The sky was cloudless and all nature had a pleasing aspect. Ruins of Inca villages, built of huge adobes or sun-dried bricks, are frequent on the slopes of the mountains. An Inca road could be traced on the other side of the valley.

Chaclacayo consists of a dozen huts built with canes from the riverside and plastered with mud. There are rose trees and jessamines, while a vine twines its branches over the verandah of the little *tambo* or inn. We did not stop and soon the road became worse, passing close along the sides of the rocky hills which bound the valley and are covered with cacti. So we journeyed on, with the great weight of silver, until we reached the small hut called Yanacocha, inhabited by one Chinese boy. A few miles farther on the valley becomes much narrower, while the road passes along the sides of perpendicular rocks with the river foaming beneath. Then the sun set, leaving a bright crimson tinge on the western sky, and soon afterwards the moon rose. It was dark when we reached a small *chacra* or farm called Santa Ana, where, to our great disgust, we found fifty mules and a dozen *arrieros* (muleteers). There was nothing to eat except what we had brought with us, some bread and bits of sausage. An *arriero*'s boy had strained the muscles of his thigh in some extraordinary way. At first I thought the bone was broken. I rubbed the place with brandy for a good long time, which eased the pain. We slept on the floor in our clothes.

Next morning Hartrick wanted to make the *arrieros* think that the bag of silver had nothing heavy in it. So he took it up as if it was a featherweight, but the heavy burden bent down his wrist and crashed down on his toe, hurting him a good deal. The *arrieros* immediately saw what was up and burst out laughing. The cat was out of the bag, which was very disagreeable as any rogues among them might attack us if they saw a chance of success.

We continued our way up the valley, which got narrower and narrower with lofty mountains on either side. In two hours we reached a hut called Ccari-chaca, and then, passing through a mile of fruit gardens, we entered the pretty little village of Cocachacra. It is situated in a lovely spot and, like the happy valley in *Rasselas* [by Samuel Johnson], surrounded by almost perpendicular mountains. On the ridges aloes and cacti grow in abundance. Through the valley flows the rapid Rimac, with orchards and gardens on its banks, fields of maize and alfalfa farther back. Here oranges, figs, *chirimoyas* [custard apples], and *paltas* [avocados] grow luxuriantly, as well as watermelons. In the pastures were cattle, horses, and sheep.

Cocachacra is a delightful little paradise. Here the people are Indians with sad mournful eyes. The women wear a shirt of coarse blue stuff, with a broad figured belt of plaited straw round the waist, white bodice trimmed with red braid, and a broad-brimmed hat. The little *tambo* where we stopped is pleasantly situated in the centre of the village with a broad verandah in front and is kept by a handsome old Indian lady. This was the point to which I had agreed to accompany Hartrick, but I went up the zigzag path beyond for some distance before wishing him farewell. He had been a very pleasant travelling companion. I never saw him again nor heard what had become of him.

I returned to Cocachacra and had a nice repast of fresh eggs, potatoes, and chocolate with milk. In the evening I walked in the fruit gardens by the river until I met a girl who refused to take any payment for all the fruit I had eaten. After sunset there was the same splendid sky as last night, almost surrounding the little valley with a crimson halo. The *tambo* in which I slept is built of large adobes and roofed with poles of the maguey, with crosspieces secured by rope made of the maguey leaf.

Next morning, after a cup of chocolate, I set out to reach Lima without stopping, except at Chaclacayo, where I had a cup of wine. Near Lima I was met by five mounted Negroes, who ranged across the road. With a pistol in each hand I rushed at them, and they made way for me grinning. I reached Lima late and went to a *tertulia* at the Codecidos.

The same gang was caught next day by a detachment of cavalry. Seven were shot and their bodies were laid out in the Plaza de la Inquisición. I went to see them and recognized three of my friends of Thursday.

My next excursion was to the famous [Indian] temple of Pachacámac, to which place old Somerville [Lieutenant Philip Somerville, commander of the *Collingwood*] had prevented me from going with my friend [John Maurice] Wemyss when I was a midshipman in the *Collingwood*. I went alone and owing to a festive luncheon at the Barredas I did not start until after two P.M. Quickly covering the ground to the watering place of Chorrillos, I pressed on round the promontory of Morro Solar and turned down into a wood of *algorrobo* trees (*prosopis horrida*) in a deep hollow. They had a weird unearthly appearance with great sprawling branches covered with cobwebs and no leaves. Passing this wood the road enters a broad and handsome avenue bordered by adobe walls and tall willow trees, which leads to the hacienda of Villa. Fruit gardens and fields of maize, alfalfa, and sugarcane spread out on either side, and the hacienda is an extensive collection of buildings, including a fine house and church, *galpón* [quarters] for 480 slaves, boiling house, and other outbuildings. The Villa slaves have a bad character, for some years ago they killed the majordomo and burnt his body in an oven. The place suffers from having an absentee owner.

Beyond Villa an extensive plain reaches to the sea and southward to the great desert of San Juan. It contains lakes frequented by wild duck and teals and swampy banks overgrown with tall canes, the haunts of sandpipers and curlew. The scenery reminded me, as it did my dear old friend Wemyss, of [Edwin Henry] Landseer's "The Widow." Passing this plain the road ascends a steep hill and enters the sandy desert of San Juan, about six miles broad. At length, from the summit of an almost imperceptible ascent, the Pacific Ocean with three rocky islets off the coast first breaks upon the view. Then the *cerro* [hill] on which stood the once splendid temple of Pachacámac is included in the panorama. Passing rapidly down the slope and skirting the little farm of Mamacona, I entered the city of the dead.

It was getting very late, so I went to a hut that was in sight to secure lodging for the night. The people promised me a supper and a night's shelter, and I returned to the ruins to explore them until dark.

The houses are built of small sun-dried bricks, but the roofs are gone and the rooms filled with sand. I ascended the *cerro* and found that the temple on the summit consisted of three broad terraces, with walls covered in some places with vermillion paint. From the platform on the top there was a glorious view. I found it to be 398 feet above the level of the sea. But I had lingered too long. After sunset it rapidly becomes dark in the tropics.

When I returned to the hut it was quite dark and the place was occupied by a gang of Negro robbers. Luckily they had unsaddled their horses and turned them into a corral (yard). One ruffian was in the road and seized my bridle. I fired my revolver at him and he dropped. Others rushed out of the hut upon me. I put spurs to my horse and galloped off into the desert, giving them two more shots. At first I intended to reach the plain of Villa and seek shelter at the hacienda. But it was quite dark and I soon lost my way. I feared I might go in a circle and come back to the hut. It ended by my passing the night in the desert, tethering the horse to one of my legs by the lasso. I slept at intervals and when at last it was sufficiently light to see my compass I found I had been riding eastward toward the mountains, away from Villa. Recovering the track, I rode briskly to Chorrillos, arriving at 7:30 A.M. Both man and beast were fam-

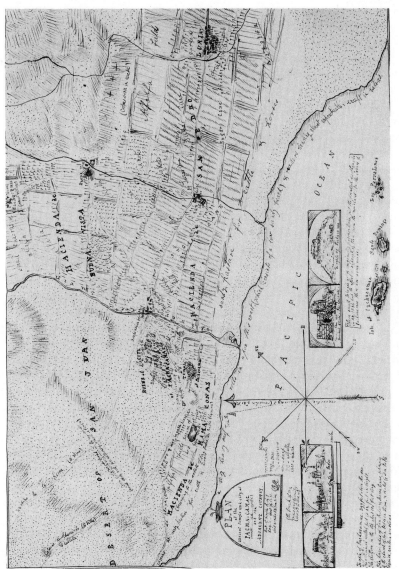

"From the platform on the top there was a glorious view."

ished and did ample justice, the one to cups of chocolate and bread, the
other to water and clover.

I ought not to have gone so late and I ought not to have gone alone. I
related my disaster at luncheon next day to Don Juan Aliaga, the count of
Lurigancho, who was very sympathetic. He offered, in the next week, to
go with me as far as Villa and to get me a good guide there to take me to
the ruins and then to the hacienda of San Pedro, which was owned by a
friend of his, to pass the night.

On the appointed day I got up early, my horse was ready, and I rode to
the Aliaga house near the Rimac bridge, where Don Juan's horse was also
waiting. We cantered off to Chorrillos, arriving very hungry, and had a
tremendous breakfast. Then we rode on to Villa. The hacienda belongs to
Señora Lavalle, Don Juan's wife's aunt. The fine estate is going to ruin
from want of proper care. There is a beautiful garden with statues and
fountains but all in a state of lamentable dilapidation, and there is a really
splendid house. The mill for crushing the sugarcane is worked by water
power, conveyed from the mountains by means of an aqueduct on arches.

Here I took leave of Don Juan Aliaga. He was a right good fellow, almost like an English country squire. His chief fault is that his ruling passion is gambling. The Aliagas are one of the noblest families in Peru, descended from a very eminent statesman named Navamuel, who was
secretary to successive viceroys in the latter part of the sixteenth century.

At Villa I was supplied with an excellent guide, a trustworthy slave on
the Villa estate. We reached Pachacámac early so that I had time to investigate the ruins thoroughly, and I took a round of angles. I then went to
my friend at the hut. He told me that between my visits a band of robbers
had arrived and taken possession for the night. He had no chance of
warning me. Next day they robbed ten mule drivers and a gentleman on
their way to Lurín. I had wounded one, whom they carried off.

There is a handsome iron bridge here for the floods, built by the enterprising owner of the hacienda of San Pedro, which is close by, a very extensive sugar farm with a steam engine for crushing the cane with marvellous rapidity. I was most cordially received by Don Pablo Elguera, who
is not an actual owner but rents the estate from the church of San Pedro
at Lima for $6,000 a year. The engineer was a Yorkshireman and at once
guessed that I was one also, "because I looked so wholesome." Don Pablo
gave me a splendid luncheon. I then went on to the village of Lurín and to
the hacienda of Buenavista. The house there is perched on an isolated
rock and has arcades all round it, a most picturesque object. Here I took
a round of angles to combine with those taken at Pachacámac and Lurín.

After a pleasant evening at San Pedro, I was shown into a very large
bedroom upstairs. Some little Negro boys slept in the passage outside. In
the middle of the night there was the most tremendous earthquake I ever

experienced. I found the little boys by my bedside, come to see what I would do. I thought the house was coming down but I was too sleepy to get up, hoping that the second shock would be slight. My hope was fulfilled and we all went to sleep again.

Next day, after breakfast, I took leave of Don Pablo and returned to Lima, after a friendly parting with my guide at Villa.

I made a fourth excursion from Lima with Mr. Pearson, the chaplain, with the object of examining the huge mounds called *huacas,* in the valley of the Rimac, on both sides of the road between Lima and the sea. They are vast artificial hills built of small adobe bricks, rising from a perfectly level plain. They are of enormous size. One of them, near the village of Magdalena, covers more than an acre and is seventy feet high. It is generally supposed from the immense quantity of skulls and bones that have been dug up that they were merely burial places. I am of opinion that they answered a much more extensive purpose. Doubtless a part of the great mass was used for sepulture, but I think that their principal object was to afford protection to the lord of the valley and his people in the event of invasion; also to supply, from their height, a more salubrious dwelling place and a post whence to overlook the cultivation.

At the bases of the *huacas* there is generally a collection of ruins built of enormous adobes and frequently a court enclosed by a high wall, resembling the present *galpones* or villages of the slaves on the sugar estates. They were probably used as habitations for troops and attendants. The date of the *huacas* is long previous to the conquest of the valley of the Rimac by the Incas, though built by people of the same race.

The time had now come for starting on my more extended travels; indeed, I fear that I had lingered too long at Lima.

Chapter 4

Lima to Cañete

AT LAST all was ready for starting on my long journey. General Torrico had kindly told off a cavalry soldier to go with me as far as Cañete. I left my heavy luggage in the care of M. Morin, and the whole of my worldly goods were to be carried in a pair of *alforjas* [packs] and a pair of leather saddlebags.

Clothes on: felt hat, shooting coat, waistcoat, fustian trousers, Arctic shirt, flannel waistcoat, drawers, cotton socks, boots, leggings, handkerchief, pocket handkerchief, poncho, spurs;

Clothes packed: black coat, black waistcoat, black trousers, plaid trousers, nankeen trousers, three check shirts, one white shirt, two Arctic shirts, three flannel waistcoats, three pairs of drawers, two pairs of woollen socks, four pairs of cotton socks, six pocket handkerchiefs, four handkerchiefs, one warm muffler, two towels, gloves, purse, Panama hat, cap, thick shoes, thin shoes;

Arms: two pistols, one revolver, one long knife, one life preserver, ammunition;

Toilet: hair brush, comb, toothbrush, nail brush, button hook, scissors, soap, two bottles eau de cologne, vinaigrette;

Books: Bible, prayer book, Spanish grammar, Spanish dictionary, nautical almanac, mathematical tables, [Archibald] Alison's *Essays [on the Nature and Principles of Taste]*;
Instruments: watch, azimuth compass, sextant, artificial horizon, aneroid, thermometer, hygrometer, telescope;
In letter case: lucifers, pocket book, ink, seals, sealing wax, pens, penknife, ruler, square, compasses, pencils, Indian ink, string;
In portfolio: foolscap, drawing paper, note paper, envelopes, letters, five notebooks, two drawing books;
Food: one pot for hot water, two packets of tea, eighteen biscuits, three pots of sardines, liquor flask, knife, spoon, and fork, housewife given me by Lady Milner;
A walking stick;
Mule gear, riding: one *sudador* [blanket], one *corona*, one saddle, one *pellón* [blanket], one pair of holsters, stirrup leathers, stirrups, one lasso, one bridle and bit with long thong, one pair of eye blinders, one *retranca* (crupper), one *hacena*, one whip;
Mule gear, cargo: one *sudador*, two blankets, one thick poncho, one *corona*, one *pellón*, one saddle, stirrup leathers and stirrups, one lasso, one bridle and bit with long thong, one pair of eye blinders, one *retranca*, one *hacena*, two *alforjas*, one pair of leather saddlebags.

The spare saddle for the cargo mule was in case I wanted to mount a guide or boy; otherwise *arrieros* were to find their own mounts. Money in gold was sewn up in a leather belt round my waist; small change in the purse. I never smoked.

The saddlebags were carefully packed and a Chinese boy was to take them to the corral where the mules were. The soldier made his appearance mounted on his horse with sword and musket, and we all made our way across the bridge to the corral. The soldier saddled my mule, the Bdellium, and loaded the other. We then set out, but it was late in the afternoon and I determined to sleep at Chorrillos. Trotting diagonally across the great square, followed by the soldier leading the cargo mule, I met Colonel Almonte, who asked me if I was going to *pasear* [ride] as far as Magdalena (three miles). "No! to Cuzco" (300 miles), I replied. "¡Caramba! ¡Dios guarda vos [God keep you]!" he cried, throwing his arms up in unfeigned surprise.

We left Lima by the Guadalupe gate and the first disaster took place about three miles further on, opposite the *fábrica de ladrillos* (brick works). The girth of the saddlebags carried away and the whole cargo fell down amidst the derisive laughter of three women on donkeys and a Negro boy. I got things to rights temporarily; but my suspicions were confirmed that my military friend was endowed with very small mental development, was devoid of common sense, and that all his fingers were thumbs. He was not to be trusted in saddling or loading. Of all the Peruvian crossbreeds, I at first put him down as a *zambo* [of Indian and black descent], but I believe he was only a *mulatto* [of black and white descent]. His age was twenty-three; his name José Mellena. I arrived late at the Chorrillos hotel, which was kept by a Frenchman and frequented by gamblers and loafers. During the night my sleep was much disturbed by bell ringing, drumming, muskets, and crackers (being the eve of the feast of the Conception), besides the crowing of numerous gamecocks.

Next day, being December 8, I thoroughly repaired all damage and started at noon. I rode the Cotham this time, the Bdellium being the cargo mule. Just beyond the Morro Solar a passing Negro told my warrior, who had been drinking, something about robbers. He got into a great fuss and began to load his musket, which, by the way, was marked "Tower G[eorge] III R [ex]." A Negro came up during the operation on a donkey and stopped to greet me, being my old Villa friend who guided me to Pachacámac. Then that ass of a soldier insisted on showing us the scars he had received in conflicts with robbers. It was three P.M. before we reached the desert. Unluckily, I had let the warrior load the Bdellium, and just as we got on the sand the whole cargo turned round under its belly. It kicked lustily and tried to run away. It took me some time to get things put to rights. We passed by Pachacámac and the hacienda of San Pedro without stopping and reached the village of Lurín at six P.M.

I put up at the house of Mariano Lásquez, the schoolmaster, who supplied me with a good supper and gave up his bedroom to me. Among his few books was *Robinson Crusoe* in Spanish, first translated in 1847. Next morning about two dozen little boys came to school in the *patio* or court, which was made into a flower garden. I took a walk in the very pretty gardens and fields toward the seashore and bathed in the little river. The terraces of the Pachacámac temple were in sight over the willow trees. The schoolmaster gave me a letter of introduction to his uncle, the baker at Chilca, the next village down the coast, and I started at two P.M. As to saddling and loading, my final words to the warrior were, "Never again!"

About two miles beyond Lurín we passed Jaguay, a little fishing port, and the desert commences again, covered with the bones of mules and donkeys. A spur of rocky hills runs from the sierra to the sea, ending in a lofty headland. The road passes over these hills which are in some places covered with cacti. It was curious to see the turkey buzzards sitting on the rocks airing themselves, with their wings spread out to the full extent. From the hills the plain of Chilca came in sight, a sandy waste with a ribbon of bright green crossing it from the sierra to the sea. The towers of Chilca church rise conspicuously over the trees.

I went to the house of José Chumpitasy and was most hospitably received by the worthy baker and his pretty daughter, who gave me an excellent supper. The house looked terribly dilapidated outside but was not really so bad. I was shown into a decent bedroom, which, though it had no roof to speak of and a mud floor, possessed a bedstead and clean sheets, which were more important in a rainless climate.

The baker had gone away on business before I got up, leaving his daughter to entertain me. After breakfast I went out to see the place. The house is in one corner of the plaza near the very fine church. That morning was the feast of our Lady of Loreto and a procession consisting of a priest in his robes, a great cross, a little table carried by four men and covered with artificial flowers, and three boys with crackers marched round the plaza.

After luncheon I took a walk toward the sea. The soil is sandy but there are many palm, pomegranate, and fig trees. The only moisture is obtained by digging wells. Several places had also been excavated to get water and surrounded by low stone walls where reeds were cultivated to make matting for the roofs of houses. There was a little scanty herbage on sand hills and a small quantity of maize, with a well in each field. The inhabitants of Chilca are pure Indians and very industrious. The whole width of the scanty vegetation does not average more than a mile, an oasis in the desert.

Returning to the town, I found dinner ready. I was entertained by the baker's pretty daughter, who is a very nice girl. It was engaging to see her cross herself and say a little prayer when the vesper bell rang. We conversed pleasantly together until ten P.M., when I went to bed.

I was awakened next morning by my military friend rushing into my room with a drawn sword, followed by the male population of Chilca, all talking at the same time. There was I in bed, so, after obtaining silence, I held a *lit de justice*. It appeared that the soldier had been on the loose all night, and in the morning the syndic asked him for his passport and slapped him in the face. The syndic denied the blow. Then the soldier fetched the village official a crack on the head with one of my pistols, which he had no business to touch. The whole village immediately got into a violent state of excitement. Headed by the governor in a large cloak and carrying a gold-headed stick, the people rushed into my bedroom. The syndic soon followed in a furious passion, with his head bandaged up, a very red face, and a blue poncho. They wanted to send the warrior bound to Lima. To this I objected. After much talk I at last induced them to be satisfied with a report being sent to the minister of war. The culprit was insolent both to the governor and the syndic until I made use of some violent language. I then politely requested the male population to retire, so as to enable me to get up and dress. The row lasted a long time and it was not until one P.M. that I was able to bid farewell to my kind young hostess, who absolutely refused to take any payment.

The road after leaving Chilca passes over a sandy waste with the striking promontory of Chilca Point to the right. It then crosses a range of hills near the sea. At one place a number of people were fishing in a little sandy bay. Turning the point of a hill, we came in sight of the beautiful vale of Mala. We descended into the plain and passed along a road bordered by bananas, figs, oranges, and fields of maize, with many tall willow trees. Vines were also cultivated near the hills. Half a mile further on was the little village of San Antonio, with a chapel embedded in fruit trees. Then we came to the river of the same name which fertilizes this delightful valley. It was tremendously swollen, the water coming up to the mules' bellies and nearly carrying them off their legs. Ascending a hill and passing through about a mile more of fertile and well cultivated land, we entered the little town of Mala when it was nearly dark and arrived at the house of the very hospitable *cura* [priest], Don Martín Fernández, for whom I had a letter. The houses in Mala have broad verandahs with pillars of cane, neatly whitewashed.

Soon after my arrival the old *cura*, after having shown me my room, announced that dinner was ready. We were joined by Don Rafael, the doctor. Both the old gentlemen had excellent appetites and did full justice to the dishes of duck, fowl, *chupé* [stew], *camarones* [shrimps], and *dulces* [sweets.]. The repast was concluded with cups of thick chocolate and glasses of water. Then there was a long grace.

The conversation of the old *cura* was very interesting. He told me that his house was on the site of the place where the famous interview took place [in November 1537] between Pizarro and Almagro about the boundary of their respective governments. It was an Inca building which had been fitted up for the meeting of the hostile chiefs. Dr. Fernández had found remains of the ancient building. Treachery was intended and one of Almagro's friends hummed two lines of an old song under a window: "Tiempo es de andar caballero / Tiempo es de andar de aquí" [It's time to leave sir / It's time to leave here]. Almagro heard and understood it, left the room on some pretence, mounted his horse, and galloped away.

After a very comfortable night's rest, I got up at eight on December 12 and found an excellent breakfast ready, as good and plentiful as the dinner. Then I took leave of the two warm-hearted old gentlemen, loth to part with them and to leave their beautiful valley.

The road to the south passes the large hacienda of Bujama belonging to Don José Asín, where there are extensive pastures and large herds of cattle. It is from here that the bulls are supplied for the Lima bull-ring. Beyond is another waste of heavy sand, but soon we came in sight of the

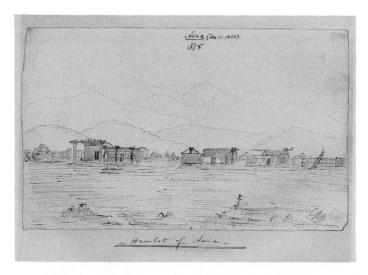

"It was a weird place. The huts . . . had a gnarled and twisted appearance."

plain of Asia, a tract of sand with a few small bushes and half a dozen huts. Here we stopped as I wanted to get some sights and observe for the variation. It was a weird place. The huts, built of crooked poles of the *algorrobo,* had a gnarled and twisted appearance. Behind them were a few fields of pumpkins and fig trees, the maritime cordillera forming a background with peaks hidden in the clouds. After taking my observations I went to the seashore and took a long walk along the hard, smooth sands. I found a sandy hill covered with human skulls and bones, with fragments of pottery and woven cotton. Not having had a bath since Lurín, I stripped and went into the surf, which was a dangerous thing to do for it was with difficulty that I struggled on shore again, owing to the undertow. I then remembered that a poor boy of the *America* was drowned in that way during the cricket match with the *Collingwood* in 1845 at Bellavista.

My host was the governor of Asia, living in one of the weird huts. He had married a Negress and had two very saucy daughters. Dinner was at four P.M. and consisted of an excellent *chupé* made of chickens, eggs, and potatoes with some other vegetables. Afterwards I took a long walk inland, far beyond the pumpkin fields toward the mountains. The strange place rather fascinated me.

In the evening a neighbour came in to drink *pisco* [brandy] with us. He had been a soldier and gave me very amusing accounts of the battles of Ingavi and Agua Santa.[1] He had two volumes of the *Comentarios Reales* of Garcilaso de la Vega. Hitherto I had only known the translation by Sir

Paul Rycaut. It was truly a strange place to find them, and I sat up reading far into the night. Then I slept among my *pellón* and blankets.

I took leave of the dweller in the weird hut and his saucy daughters early in the morning of December 13 and set out for Cañete. My military escort had been very piano and anxious to please since the row at Chilca. After crossing a barren waste we reached the Cañete Valley. Passing across the yard of the Hacienda de Quebrada we went down a road bounded on either side by fields of sugarcane and came to the Hacienda de Huaca, where I was to stop.

Next day the warrior set out on his return to Lima. I gave him a letter to General Torrico, thanking His Excellency for all his kindness. The poor soldier was not a bad chap on the whole, so I inadvertently forgot to report the row at Chilca.

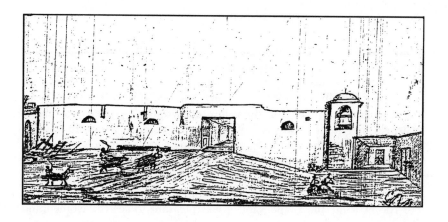

Chapter 5

Cañete

MY HOST at the Hacienda de Huaca at Cañete was Don Mariano de Osma, brother of the Señora Barreda. His brother, Don Ignacio José de Osma, is a statesman and diplomatist. There is also a flourishing branch of the family in Spain. The actual owner of the estate is a relative, Doña Josefa Ramírez de Asellano de Osma. Don Mariano is a very nice young fellow, as yet unmarried. As a host nothing could equal his hospitality and anxiety to please and amuse me. He introduced me to the *administrador,* a quaint old gentleman, and then to his wife, called Mamita by the slaves, who was sitting in her apartment sewing with her maids. She asked me how long I had been coming and I replied, "Six days." She cried out, "¡Jesús, María, y José!" I explained I was in no hurry, that I wanted to see the country, and that I had observations to take. She simply repeated very emphatically as if there was no more to be said, "¡Jesús, María, y José!" Ever afterwards whenever she got a chance she said, "Don Clemente requires time."

The house, with a wide verandah, faces a large courtyard with the crushing house opposite. On the two other sides are the entrance gate and Mamita's rooms to the north and other offices to the south. The hacienda is built over an ancient *huaca,* hence the name. Behind the house, at the foot of this artificial hill, on the side toward the sea is the garden containing a running stream and vines, citrons, oranges, bananas, *chirimoya,* and *palta* trees. In a small enclosure are peaches, granadillas, sweet peas, roses, jessamine, pinks, and the beautiful *floripondio.* There was also a peacock. The house consisted of the *administrador's* room, the dining room opening to the verandahs at both ends, Don Mariano's room, and the office turned into my room, both spacious and lofty apartments. For reading in bed I had a novel called *El Duque de Azevada* and a book of travels in Peru by a Chilean named Vicuña who visited Cañete.[1] Next to our rooms came the chapel, and it was pleasant to see the women and girls kneeling at the chapel door and hear them singing at matins and vespers. All was on the ground floor.

Our breakfast was at ten. They got up very early but never touched anything until then. There were three little Negro boys named Juan, Anaclito, and Simoncito to fan the flies off and keep up a current of air. Manuel was a bigger boy who waited on Don Mariano and me and waited at dinner, a capital fellow. The party consisted of Don Mariano, the *administrador,* Mamita, a girl named Dolores, and me. But the *administrador* usually stood about, watching to see when anyone had finished, and crying out, "Quitate plato" [Remove the plate]. The first dish at breakfast was a *caldo* or gravy soup. Next came a dish of poached eggs, done round with slices of fried banana, then some ribs of mutton with rice and *frijoles* (beans), finishing with a cup of well-frothed chocolate. Dinner was at four, sometimes later. The first dish was an excellent *chupé,* then a dish of fish in vinegar and *ají* [chili pepper], followed by cutlets done with fried breadcrumbs, then a dish of very young *ají* with potatoes, tamarinds done with suet, *camotes* [yams] with sugar made into a sort of sticky jam pudding, then a delicious sort of *dulce,* some preserved fruits, finishing with a glass of water. In the evening there was a cup of chocolate.

The view from Huaca is one great level of sugarcane in all directions, with willow trees lining the hedges. Toward the sea is Cerro Azul, the port of Cañete, and there are two small towns, Pueblo Viejo and Pueblo Nuevo.

Besides maize and alfalfa farms near the mountains there are eight sugar haciendas in the Cañete Valley: Quebrada, rented by Mr. W. Reid and Mr. Swayne at Lima, owned by the Convent of Buenamuerte; Casa Blanca, rented by Mr. Reid (Mr. Reswick, manager), also owned by Buenamuerte; Huaca, owned by Don Mariano de Osma; Santa Barbara, owned by Don Domingo Carrillo; San Juan de Arona, owned by Don Pedro Paz Soldán;[2] Montalván, owned by Don Demetrio O'Higgins, natural son of the Chilean general to whom it was granted when he was banished and who died there; Gomes, owned by Don Juan Unanue

(Manuel Samudio, manager), whose sister married Pedro Paz Soldán; and Hualcará, owned by Don Antonio Ramos. Here there is a steam engine with a vacuum pan by which the sugar is boiled.

In the whole valley there are about two thousand Negro slaves. They live in villages with huts built round a plaza, generally with a cross in the centre. The villages are surrounded by high walls and all must be within by a certain hour. There is one entrance. The slave-walled village is called a *galpón* and each hacienda has one, besides a chapel and a *cura*. The *cura* of Huaca was rather morose. He never joined us at breakfast or dinner but came for a cup of chocolate at nine P.M. He is a little old Spaniard named Antonini, with a pale face, aquiline nose, and sparkling eyes, and his words come out beautifully distinct and clear. On December 17 he was confessing a large gang of Negresses all the afternoon, and again on the 18th he was catechizing boys in the chapel.

I liked all the black people I came in contact with. The women and children are cared for and their religious instruction is attended to. Hitherto the Peruvian government has wisely avoided extremes in dealing with the slave question and has adopted a scheme of gradual emancipation. In 1821 a law was passed that all slaves who were then slaves would be slaves for life. Children born after 1821 were to be free at the age of fifty. Their children were to be born free.[3] It was intended that the Negroes should become gradually accustomed to liberty; and at the same time the slave owners would have a period of preparation by employing machinery and procuring Chinese labour to make up for the loss of some of the Negroes. It was thought that few would desert their homes where they have been well treated from childhood, when their condition had been improved by freedom and receipt of pay.

Opposite the house at Huaca, on the other side of the courtyard, is the crushing house. Here the cane is crushed by mules and bullocks fastened to capstan bars and driven round three capstans which turn the crushing rollers. The juice runs down a gutter into a receptacle in another long room where it is boiled. There are seven copper caldrons about six feet in diameter where the juice is boiled with furnaces underneath. Then some of it is refined, some made into brown sugar, and some into *chancaca*, cakes much eaten by the poor people. The foam and refuse of the first boiling is skimmed and put in bags, which are put under a screw press, and the juice makes an inferior sort of sugar.

The process will be better understood by reference to [the operations at San Juan de Arona. Here] the cane (*caña*) is brought into the crushing house (*trapiche*) on donkeys and brought on to the right-hand side of the crushing machine. A water wheel which is twenty-eight feet in diameter is worked by the water in a channel and turns the crushing machine, which consists of three heavy iron rollers. A number of Negroes feed the rollers

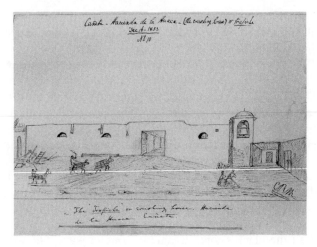

"Opposite to the house . . . is the crushing house. Here the cane is crushed by mules and bullocks . . ."

with cane and others take it away with every particle of juice crushed out. It is taken by a door into the yard and makes excellent fuel for the furnaces. Meanwhile the juice (*caldo*) runs down a channel into the boiling house. Another crushing machine with perpendicular rollers is worked by mules. The boiling house contains six caldrons (*fondos*) (about six feet in diameter and very thick) in which the juice is boiled. Each one is attended by a Negro with a long pole and a shallow calabash fastened to the end, with which he skims the foam and froth and pours it into *sachaceras*[?]. It is then taken away and put into cotton bags, which are put under the screw press, and the juice, called *cachaca*, runs into copper receptacles, leaving all the dirt and refuse in the bags. The *cachaca* makes an inferior kind of sugar.

The juice in the copper *fondos*, when it is sufficiently boiled, is allowed to run by a channel into the coolers (*enfriaderas*), where it remains for twenty-four hours. It is then let by a channel into two other *fondos*, where it is boiled again. It is then, while boiling, poured by Negroes with long poles and deep calabashes at the ends into vessels, which are carried by others across the room, and the juice is finally deposited in jars of clay made in the shape of a sugarloaf, where it is allowed to cool. This becomes a coarse brown sugar. Some of it is taken into the refining house (*casa de purga*), where the *hornos* are filled one-third with fine clay (*barro*), which purges the sugar. It remains thus for about a fortnight, all the refuse is extracted, and it becomes white sugar.

At two P.M. on December 14 I mounted the Bdellium and went with

Don Mariano to the Hacienda de Quebrada, where Mr. Reid is the superintendent, to whom I had a letter. Quebrada is now worked by a water-mill but they are setting up a steam engine lately sent out from England and landed at Cerro Azul. (There is about $100,000 worth of British ironwork in the Cañete Valley.) They are also putting up a distillery for making rum. All the indoor work is done by Chinese at four dollars a month. On the night of the 13th they had a grand funeral for one of them, whom they buried in a sand hill about a league away, leaving a dozen tapers burning over the grave. There are six Englishmen at Quebrada, namely Mr. Reid, a clerk, smith, carpenter, engineer, and bricklayer. There are also three priests, the regular *cura*, who has been there for years, the prelate of the convent of Buenamuerte, who had come here (as owner) to settle some dispute about a stream of water, and his chaplain, a young and handsome man. The monks of Buenamuerte wear a long black gown with broad red crosses on the breast and shoulder. The prelate has a high lace cap, I suppose the cendress[?] of a mitre. We returned to Huaca for dinner.

On the 15th Don Mariano and I rode over to the Hacienda de Casa Blanca, which is also rented by Mr. Reid and managed by a very dry Scotchman named Renwick. The indoor work is here also done by Chinese and the crushing by water power. They also make a good deal of rum in the distillery here and have excellent clay for making moulds for loaf sugar. A little northwest of the hacienda is a very extensive *huaca* with great quantities of human skulls and some very interesting curiosities, including mummies, pottery, and silver *canopas*.

Canopa is a household god, like the penates of the Romans. They were made of gold, silver, clay, and *quicu* or bezoar stones. The Peruvian *canopas* had the word *mama* (mother) added to the word for the thing the *canopa* represented, as *sara* (maize) *mama*, *coca mama*, *llama mama*. The latter had a hole in the back to receive offerings. This half deification of natural objects is founded on the idea of maternity or the archetype or spiritual essence of things.

The cane in Cañete is cut once in about eighteen months as the weather is cold in winter and it never rains. There is, therefore, much labour in irrigating the fields. But though the cane is slow in growing, there is more sugar in the same quantity of cane here than in many more favoured regions, the cane being harder and containing much more juice. The refined sugar at Casa Blanca is very white and hard, the refiner being a German. Nearly all the sugar that is embarked in small coasting vessels at Cerro Azul goes to Chile. The sugar for Lima goes up in long troops of mules, carrying thirteen *arrobas* (325 pounds) each.[4] The willow, almost the only timber in Cañete, grows to a great size and is very useful for many purposes.

We returned to Huaca at five P.M. and found Mr. Reid and the old prelate of Buenamuerte come to call. The latter wanted to make us believe that one of his order had fasted for forty days and forty nights, first contending that it was quite possible, and then falling back on "una obra de gracia pues" [a test of faith then].

On the 16th we went to dine at Quebrada at 5:30 P.M. We sat down eleven: Mr. Reid, the prelate, his chaplain, the *cura* of the hacienda, Don Mariano, Don Pedro Paz Soldán, the *administrador,* the clerk, the engineer, the refiner, and myself. It was a very pleasant dinner, plenty of wine, ice, and all the delicacies of the season. A spirited and interesting conversation was kept up continuously. We returned at nine P.M., Don Pedro riding with us.

On Sunday the 19th we dined with Don Pedro Paz Soldán at his Hacienda de San Juan de Arona, nicknamed Mataratones from the number of rats that have been killed. Don Pedro's brother, Don José Gregorio Paz Soldán, was for some time president of the council of state. Don Pedro is a very agreeable and intelligent country gentleman. He cannot talk English but reads it perfectly, for I got him to take an English book and translate half a page into Spanish, which he did without a mistake. He is building a splendid corridor in front of the house, a tower forty feet high for the chapel to contain a peal of five bells, and a handsome stone arch as an entrance to the courtyard. The house is handsomely furnished and the dinner was excellent.

The party consisted of Mr. Reid; the prelate; M. Marcial, the *administrador* of Montalván; Don Mariano and myself; Don Domingo Carrillo; Don Antonio Ramos; the *cura* of the hacienda; our *cura* at Huaca named Antonini; his brother; and the refiner. There was sparkling champagne and sparkling conversation. Afterwards there was a cock fight in the plaza of the *galpón,* and the old prelate got into a tremendous state of excitement, betting high with M. Marcial. Later he was playing high at *écarté* all the evening, rather unusual, it is to be hoped, for a dignitary of the church on Sunday. We got back to Huaca at eleven P.M.

On Monday, December the 20th, we dined with Don Pedro again; and on Wednesday, the 22d, we rode to the Hacienda de Montalván, which is worked by water and seems in a flourishing condition. Here the subprefect of the province, Don Juan Bautista Gallego, lives. We afterwards called on the governor of the little town of Pueblo Nuevo de Cañete, Don Mariano Salaverry, brother of the supreme chief [Felipe Santiago Salaverry], who [in 1836] was shot at Arequipa by order of General [Andrés de] Santa Cruz. We also called on the judge.

On the 24th we rode over to the pretty little town of Pueblo Viejo de Cañete, which is on the way to Cerro Azul, to see the fireworks and preparations for Christmas. The plaza was lighted up, squibs and crackers flying in all directions, for two hours.

On Christmas Day we all went to Pueblo Viejo for a regular burst. Don Mariano rode his horse and I was on the Cotham. Mamita and the three girls, Dolores, Nicolasita, and Anaclita, each had a donkey, the maids, Juanita and Simona, had one between them. The boys, Manuel, Juan, Anaclito, and Simoncito, were all on one donkey. I lent the Bdellium to the Indian carpenter from Yauyos, aged about eighteen and named Antonino. Don Mariano and I headed the jovial and rather noisy procession.

We were in plenty of time for high mass at the church of Pueblo Viejo, where the prelate of Buenamuerte and the *curas* of Pueblo Viejo, Huaca, and Quebrada officiated. Our *cura* of Huaca preached a long extemporary sermon on the worship of the Virgin Mary, clearly and eloquently delivered.

After church Don Mariano and I went by previous invitation to dinner at the *cura*'s house, the prelate completing the party. The rest went for their respective larks. The dinner consisted of an excellent roast sucking pig, pastry made of young green maize, and *dulces*. After dessert the prelate of Buenamuerte took his game cock out of a basket and put it on the table. Dr. Licero, the *cura,* did the same with his and about eighteen neighbours came in. The two ecclesiastics were soon busily engaged in fastening the *navajas* (well-sharpened steel spurs) on their respective cocks. Then the battle began, feathers flew in all directions, the excitement reached fever heat, the betting rose higher and higher. In the end the cock of the sporting old prelate of Buenamuerte was victorious and much money changed hands. The conquering cock rejoiced in the name of "Pilato."

As soon as we had calmed down we adjourned to a house where there were ten young ladies who sang love songs, played on guitars, and taught me to dance the *zamacueca* until past midnight.[5] Then came the getting home again. Through the energy of Mamita and Antonino the whole party was collected in the plaza with the beasts by one A.M. We all rode home more noisily than we went, reaching Huaca at two in the morning. The whole household kissed Don Mariano's hand and we retired to rest after a very festive and enjoyable Christmas.

On the 26th there was another large dinner party at Quebrada to which we went; and on the 27th three very pretty girls, cousins of Dolores, came on a visit. We played at hide and seek and rounders in the garden all the afternoon.

The 28th of December was the day fixed for me to continue my journey to the south. After dinner we sat talking for a long time. I found difficulty in expressing my feelings of friendship and gratitude toward Don Mariano de Osma. Then Mamita brought in a sort of farewell collation, with some of her delicious *dulces*. I was fond of Mamita, though her incessant chaff about my slow rate of travelling got wearisome at times. It got dark and suddenly we found it was eight P.M. Don Mariano decided that it was much too late to go further than the Hacienda de Gomes, the most southern in the Cañete Valley. Our boy Manuel was to go with me, and at last the final farewells were said and we set out in the dark. There was a slight disaster with the cargo mule, which Manuel and I put to rights with a little difficulty, and we arrived safely at Gomes by ten P.M.

Chapter 6

Cañete to Pisco

I WAS most hospitably received at the Hacienda de Gomes, which is a large and very flourishing estate. Next morning I had to part with the Negro boy, Manuel, and bid him farewell. We had been great friends. The river which we had to cross was reported to be much swollen, so the *administrador* lent me a very tall Chilean horse to take me over dry, a man in charge of it, and a guide to take me as far as Chincha.

I left Gomes rather late. After passing the sugarcane fields of the hacienda, the road leads through small farms of maize, vegetables, alfalfa, and fruit trees until we came to the banks of the river Cañete close to its mouth. Tall reeds line its banks, above which rises a bare hill crowned by the extensive ruins of the Inca fortress of Herbay. The river was in full flood but I crossed it comfortably on the tall Chilean horse, Bdellium and Cotham following as best they could. I eagerly climbed the hill, which is about sixty feet high, forming a promontory. I spent some time making a plan of the ruins, which were, I found, in two parts separated by a sort of *place d'armes*, three hundred yards in length.

The first part is more inland than the second and consists of nine chambers. Entering by a breach in the wall on the north side, I passed along a rampart broad enough for two men to walk abreast, with a parapet five feet high on one side and the palace wall sixteen feet high on the other. The parapet is on the edge of a steep descent, partly faced with adobes. At the end of twenty yards the passage turns at right angles into the centre of the building, where there is a doorway ten feet high and three feet at the base, the sides sloping inwards as in most Inca-built edifices, with a lintel of willow beams. It led into a spacious hall, and corresponding with the doorway on the opposite wall is a recess exactly like it. The walls are sixteen feet high, built of adobes the size of ordinary bricks, if anything larger. These walls had once been plaistered over. At the sides of the hall are passages, with recesses resembling windows, communicating with small chambers. Between the ramparts are four other chambers also with recesses. The part of this edifice facing the *place d'armes* is in ruins. It is separated by three hundred yards from the other edifice, which overlooks the sea.

I entered the second part by a doorway, the lintel of which is destroyed, leading into a large hall with sides ninety-seven feet long. The sides toward the north and west were blank. That to the east contains fifteen recesses like those in the spacious hall in the first part. On the south side are two doorways leading by passages sixty-seven feet long to the end wall, with a dozen small chambers on the sides. In the upper part of the walls of the great hall the holes were visible for the beams supporting the roof. The small chambers were surrounded by recesses. The walls throughout are three to five feet thick. The fortress and palace of Herbay are certainly of Inca work, built to overawe the people of the rich valley of Huarcu, afterwards called Cañete. About 170 yards to the south are the ruins of a small Inca pueblo, the houses being built of enormous adobes.

Leaving these interesting ruins, I entered a sandy waste and travelled over it for several hours, at last coming down upon the seashore by a zigzag path. The cliffs were here eighty feet high and there were a few stunted bushes at their bases. After a time the road again ascends the cliffs to a desert covered with a black kind of prickly cactus. It got quite dark and we passed through the little village of Chincha at nine P.M. But it was ten before I reached my destination, the hacienda of Larán and abode of my kind host, Don Antonio Prada, count of Los Torres de Orán. He supplied me with a good supper and a comfortable bed.[1]

When I awoke next morning, I found myself in by far the finest hacienda I had yet seen, with a most amiable host and a good breakfast ready. In front of the house are a broad and handsome verandah and a flight of stone steps leading up from the courtyard. The rooms are lofty and furnished in good taste and there is a billiard room. The sugar mill is worked by steam. Besides Larán there are two other haciendas in the rich valley of Chincha, called San José and San Regis, both belonging to Don Fernando Carrillo, count of [Montemar y] Monteblanco. The valley is twelve miles wide and there are some large *huacas* near Larán.

I should have liked to have stayed longer and was pressed by Don Antonio to do so, but I had lingered too long at Cañete. I declined, saying that I would find my own way to Pisco and started at 12:30 P.M.

The division between the jurisdictions of Pizarro and Almagro was ordered to be a straight line west to east, drawn from a point on the coast at a certain distance from Puerto Viejo, to be fixed by the pilots. They decided that Chincha was the point in question. But Chincha is exactly in the latitude of Cuzco and the city of the Incas was claimed by Pizarro. The question was settled at last after three pitched battles, the deaths of Almagro and his son, and the assassination of Pizarro, when it no longer signified. The latitude is thirteen degrees, thirty-one minutes south. A broad straight road leads from the gates of Larán to the foot of the mountain which is in this famous latitude.

Turning from this road at right angles, I had to pass over a stony wilderness overgrown with high reeds and thorny bushes. Leaving San José on the left, I then passed through the courtyard of San Regis, crossed the river Chincha, and eventually entered the desert which separates Chincha from Pisco, more than sixteen miles broad. I had to make a long round to reach a bridge as the Pisco River was very full and I did not know about a ford. I then entered the fertile plain of Pisco covered with date palms, willows, and fruit trees and large herds of goats grazing. It soon became quite dark. Reaching the house of Don Domingo Elías at eight P.M. in the plaza of Pisco, I was very glad of a nice cup of chocolate and a comfortable bed.

The great man of Pisco is Don Domingo Elías, who owns several vineyard haciendas, makes much wine and a spirit called *pisco,* and has an interest in the guano islands. He has held high office, was once indeed in charge of the executive for a few weeks during the troubles [in 1844], and is one of the leading men of Peru. He was not at Pisco but he had sent instructions to his brother-in-law and confidential clerk, M. [Francisco] Calmet, to receive and help me in every way. Nothing could exceed his obliging civility. The house has only a ground floor built round a courtyard, but it is very comfortable.

The first thing I determined to do was to visit the Chincha Islands and see what was going on there. M. Calmet arranged things for me. In the morning of December 31 I rode down to the little port about half a mile from Pisco and embarked on board a half-decked launch called the *Andria,* manned by four Chinese and two Negroes. The distance is fourteen miles and when we were halfway it fell a dead calm. I had to sleep on

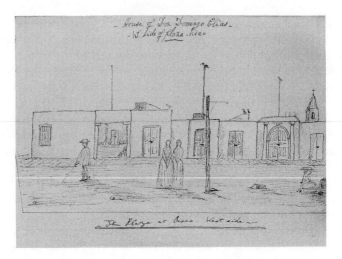

"The house has only a ground floor built round a courtyard, but it is very comfortable." Note the women wearing the *saya y manto*.

deck and we did not reach the island until midnight. I was awakened by all the merchant vessels ringing the old year out and the new year in. 1853: my age was twenty-two years, five months, ten days.

Next morning I landed by a steep ladder, which leads up the perpendicular rocks to a wooden platform formed in the side of the cliff. Thence, walking up a steep hill, I reached the house of the governor. For the last three years Don Domingo Elías has had the sole contract from the Peruvian government for shipping the guano, for which he receives 12 reales per ton of guano shipped, which is sold in England for £10. The House of Gibbs in Liverpool and Don Felipe Barreda for America also receive a percentage.

About a hundred yards from the face of the cliff is the principal cutting of guano, now full eighty feet high, where two hundred convicts were at work. There is also a small steam engine of ten or twelve horsepower for digging the guano out and filling trucks. A crane projects from the engine house with chains from which is suspended a large iron trough of about eight hundredweight, with six iron teeth at the edges. By working one chain it digs into the guano and fills itself, by connecting another the crane turns, and by another the contents of the trough are discharged into the truck. About four loads fill it, and it is drawn by a mule to the edge of the cliff, where it is emptied and shovelled down a canvas shoot into the vessel that is loading. Other men with canvas masks, who receive from the captain $13 per one hundred tons, are employed to trim the cargo in the hold. The smell of the guano is awfully strong and it is more penetrating than coal dust or steel filings. They have a tram for the trucks, from the shoot to the foot of the cutting. When I was there, twenty-five merchant vessels were anchored off the north island, besides one that was loading, but there are generally many more, sometimes over a hundred. There is also a hulk for about a dozen soldiers, who guard the convicts. The latter live in a little village built of canes and matting. There are also several houses, one for Don Jesús Elías, the son of Don Domingo; another for Zarate, the chief clerk; offices; the mess room of the employees; storerooms; a smithy with two Yorkshire blacksmiths; the houses of the Irish doctor and the priest; besides a temporary altar surrounded by canvas curtains. In addition to the principal cutting, there was one for loading boats to enable the other ships to get on loading before their turns came to go under the main shoot.

In the less frequented parts of the island there are still thousands of birds, chiefly terns, that lay their eggs in little caverns burrowed in the guano. Some of the hills are covered with these nests. Guano is a corruption of the Quechua word *huanu,* meaning manure, as *huanu huanacup* (guanaco manure), *huanu piscup* (bird manure), *huanu challuap* (fish manure), *huanu runap* (the kind mentioned in Deuteronomy 23:13).[2] The legitimate guano bird is a kind of tern, the bill and legs red, top of the head and ends of the wings black, lower part of the head white, with a long, curved, whiskerlike feather coming out from near the ear on each side, the rest of the body a dark slate colour, length from head to tip of tail about eight inches. Besides these guano terns there are pelicans, divers, and several kinds of gulls, but the terns are by far the most numerous. Some ammoniacal salts are found on the island, and the Yorkshire blacksmith gave me a petrified pelican's egg made of ammoniacal salts. The north island is about a mile and a quarter round.

At ten A.M. I returned to the houses, where old Zarate gave me a very good breakfast. He told me that Don Domingo embarked on an average about five hundred tons a day and his expenses are very small. He feeds the convicts with beans and rice from his own estates at Pisco. A launch carries provisions and water daily from the mainland. I left the island at two P.M. in the same launch and reached Pisco at sunset on New Year's Day.

During the passage I heard more abusive language in a few hours than I did in the whole time I was in Peru, for two half-caste chaps were added to the crew. Here is some of it: *carajo,* execrating exclamation; *atrevido,* audacious; *fanfarrón,* bully [braggart]; *canalla,* blackguard; *zamarro,* clodhopper; *cobarde,* coward (very insulting); *liso,* cheeky; *impávido,* impudent; *tonto,* fool; *pinganilla* or *chamberí,* snob, dandy; *palangana,* prig, charlatan; *peripuesto,* puppy; *facineroso,* bad character; *ladrón,* thief; *bribón,* scoundrel; *embustero,* liar; *zopenco,* stupid ass; *desver-*

güenza, insolent [shamelessness]; *veleta*, turncoat; *estafador*, swindler; *qué sencillo*, what a poor creature; *pillo*, rascal; *muy tonto*, very foolish; *qué disparate*, what nonsense; *qué traza*, what a figure; *pícaro*, unprincipled scoundrel; *qué bochinche*, what a row; *qué chasco*, what a sell [joke]; *cabez chascosa*, dishevelled head; *qué cándido*, what a goose; *chúcaro*, a trickster; *chuchumeca*, a free and easy young lady; *buen provecho, caballero*, much good may it do you; *no hay tonto para su provecho*, no man is a fool to his own interests. Not abusive: *Ave María purísima; Jesús, María, y José; guapo*, valiant and handsome; *pucho*, end of a cigar; *puchero*, dish composed of everything.

I was much fascinated by Pisco. There is a very fine large church in the plaza besides four others. Some good houses in the Limeñan style occur at intervals in the streets and one with two storeys in the plaza. The smaller dwellings in the outskirts are of very simple construction. Rows of canes, about eight feet high, are stuck in the ground, with crosspieces at intervals and plastered with mud. They are then whitewashed, the framework of a door put in, a glass lamp suspended from it, and a flat cane roof. It is all made to look very neat.

The Jesuits' church is still used, the high and side altars being masses of elaborately carved gilt work. Passing it, the street ends with an avenue of fine old willow trees, two little streams rippling along their roots. This leads to the gate of the suppressed monastery of Franciscans, now going to ruin. In the court of the old cloister was a pretty flower garden of sweet peas, roses, pinks, and cow parsley. The monastery is surrounded by about four acres of pleasure grounds, now neglected. The olive trees, with old gnarled trunks, are planted in avenues crossing each other at right angles, backed by oranges and fig trees. It was an extremely pleasant retreat where one could indulge in reminiscences and build castles in the air in solitude.

On the south side of Pisco the plain is quite unproductive. Stony mounds with a few stunted bushes and date palms stretch away to the desert. In some places there is a marsh where reeds are cultivated for the roofs and walls of houses. To the north it is very different. In the immediate vicinity are extensive pastures and fields of alfalfa for horses and cattle, fields of vegetables, willows, and other trees. Between Pisco and the port, on the north side of the road, is a sugar hacienda on a very small scale for making *chancaca*.

The river empties itself into the sea about a league north of the town, and on the other side, close to the beach, is the important sugar estate of Caucato, worked by steam. Further inland are the extensive vineyards of Don Domingo Elías, where immense quantities of *pisco* are made and exported to all parts of Peru and Chile, also a liqueur called "Italia," and wine. Don Domingo is the most enterprising man in Peru. He bought the broad acres of my old friend, the count of Lurigancho, for next to nothing and turned them to account; and he has shares in the Cerro de Pasco mines, in the gold mine of Huacho, and the contract for shipping the guano. His vine haciendas are Buenavista, Chacarilla, Santa Cruz, and Hoyos [La Hoya], all with vines on posts of canes tied together; Palto, formerly belonging to the Jesuits; and Urrutia, with vines on adobe pillars, formerly belonging to Don Juan Aliaga, count of Lurigancho.

On the 5th of January M. Calmet took me over Don Domingo's wine stores at Pisco, containing more than 100 butts of 280 to 300 gallons. An old and experienced Portuguese has charge of the wines and has made and clarified three very good kinds out of the Pisco and Ica grapes. One is like Málaga, another like Marsala, and the third might be mistaken for Bucellas. The best Italia is made of a large white grape and is delicious. The *chirimoya pisco* is also very grateful to the palate. Common *pisco* is stored in a large warehouse at the port.

Early in the morning of January 6 I took leave of hospitable M. Calmet and started for Ica, guided by an Indian servant, who led my cargo mules.

Chapter 7

Ica to Nazca

ICA IS separated by a range of barren hills from the sea. After leaving
Pisco, we had first to pass over two miles of heavy sand. We then entered
the hacienda of Sapo belonging to Señor Pedemonte, a cousin of Don
Domingo, which is surrounded by date palms, and came next to the hacienda of La Hoya, also abounding in palms. When the liberating fleet
arrived at Pisco from Chile, Lord [Thomas] Cochrane landed with ten
men to reconnoiter. He narrowly escaped being captured by a royalist
force of seven hundred men by climbing up a palm tree at the hacienda of
La Hoya, which is still called "Palma de Cochrane."

Beyond La Hoya the desert of heavy sand stretches away inland with
an occasional thorn tree or stunted bush. After several leagues we arrived
at the ruined hacienda of Villacuri, the oasis between Pisco and Ica. It is a
forest of date palms with fig trees and vines, all growing out of loose
sand. The hacienda was for making soap from a plant which grows in the
sand and contains much potash. Starting from Villacuri, I had not gone
very far when I discovered that my *alforjas* were missing. I sent my Indian
servant back to Villacuri for them, following more slowly with my cargo
mule and his spare horse. They, however, effected their escape and fled

away in different directions over the desert. The desert is here covered with salt in great lumps, which made it excessively difficult to ride over. After superhuman efforts under a burning sun, I at length captured them both. On returning to Villacuri there was no Indian and no *alforjas*. But in their place was Don Manuel Frías, subprefect of Ica, on his way to Lima with a secretary, orderly, and servants and a good luncheon spread on the ground, to which he invited me. There were cold fowls, ham, biscuits, *dulces*, and *chirimoya pisco*. I made it look very small and they complimented me on my appetite. It was not until six P.M. that the Indian returned to Villacuri. He had chased some people and caught them up just outside Pisco with my *alforjas*. They said they had taken them by mistake. The Indian's energy saved them. Good man!

I had to sleep among the date palms of Villacuri, starting for Ica next day at four A.M. Riding over a flat plain for five leagues and over two leagues of sand hills, we arrived at the beginning of the vale of Ica, which first shows itself in a number of stunted *algorrobo* trees, called here *huarangos,* which gradually become larger and at last form a thick wood. This tree, sometimes of great size, forms the very hardest wood possible, which by its own weight bends the trunk down, twists it round and round, and makes the branches tie overhand knots in themselves and the tree assume the most fantastic forms imaginable. Beyond the wood we passed through the courtyard of the hacienda of Macacona, owned by Don Gregorio Falconi. Half a league more, through vineyards and cotton plantations lined with fig trees, jessamine, and roses, brought us to the town of Ica, capital of the province of the same name.

I had introductions to Don Juan de Dios Quintana, the principal person, brother-in-law of Don Domingo Elías, and also to M. Calmet's relative, Don José Blas Santos Martínez. M. Calmet advised me to go to the latter as Señor Quintana would probably be absent, which indeed was the case. I was received most cordially by Señor Martínez and the Señora. There were also some very nice children. The house had a courtyard, with the living rooms facing the entrance. I was given a very comfortable bedroom opening on the courtyard.

During the day I made all my preparations for continuing my journey farther south as far as Nazca and found travelling companions. I was going in very light marching order, leaving the Cotham and half my things in the care of Señor Martínez. We were to start next day.

Ica is a large town situated six or eight miles from the foot of the cordillera and some thirty from the sea, with a barren range of hills intervening. It contains four churches and several handsome, well-furnished houses, especially that of Don Juan de Dios Quintana in the plaza. The town has suffered much from earthquakes, especially in 1745, when it was entirely destroyed. In the evening I went to the alameda with the

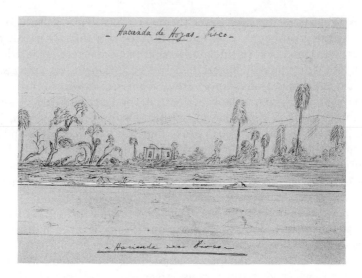

" . . . the hacienda of La Hoya, also abounding in palms."

Martínez family. From the plaza a street leads down to the river, which is crossed in this season by a bridge of ropes and willow that bends to and fro. During the greater part of the year the river is dry. In January and February the water dashes impetuously down the valley, the bed being lined with tall willow trees. Here the ladies of Ica have their chairs brought out and sit talking in the cool of the evening. An avenue of willows leads down to a small house which is surrounded by fruit trees, the majestic Andes rising behind. We passed a very pleasant evening.

Next morning after breakfast, my travelling companions came to see me. They were Don José Cintura and Mr. Isaac Ladd, an American who had been employed by Don Domingo Elías as an engineer for thirteen years. He was going down to the coast to load a ship with bales of cotton, which were already on the beach. I thought this would be good fun and an incident in my journey to the south. We did not start until the evening of January the 8th.

The valley of Ica is covered with cotton plantations, vineyards, and every kind of fruit and vegetable. The vines are raised on poles of *huarango* wood. There are three mills for cleaning cotton in the valley, one of them belonging to Don Domingo Elías, who has two cotton estates here, La Tinguiña and Ocucaje, where we were to pass the night. The road crosses the river and then, passing Don Pedro Toledo's hacienda of San Ramón, enters a dense wood of *huarango* trees, many of them arching over the road, which continues all the way. Occasionally we passed a hut built of *huarango* and consequently assuming a corkscrew-like appearance. At nine P.M. we arrived at the cotton hacienda of Ocucaje. The *administrador*, Don Agustín Lobos, had cups of chocolate ready for us, and so to bed.

We started at eleven A.M. on the 9th and it was necessary to cross the river of Ica again. Mr. Ladd went first and I followed. I had hardly got halfway when the stream, which was shallow but very strong, carried the Bdellium off his legs and threw him on his side with my leg under him so I could not get my head above water to breathe. The mule kicked and struggled and so did I, and at length we were extricated, drenched through and through. The only permanent injury was that my fustian trousers became partly blue from the dye which came off my *pellón*.

The road on the other side passes through half a league of cotton plantation, lined by hedges of *huarango* and an acacia with deliciously sweet leaves and flowers. We then entered the sandy desert, which extends for forty miles to the sea. There are several curiously shaped conical hills stratified horizontally, one called Cerro de Brujas (Hill of Witches), but the road is a long and weary one. It was not until nine P.M. that we descended a long, steep cliff and arrived at the little hut built of bamboos from Guayaquil, which forms the seaport of Lomas [Lomitas]. That night I slept on cotton bales and in the morning we began to load the barque, *Jenny Lind* of London, with cotton. Many bales were piled on the beach. The cotton is brought down on mules, each one carrying two bales weighing 175 pounds each. There is a considerable surf at Lomas and we had to embark the cotton on a large raft made of the wood of the cabbage tree from Guayaquil. Don Domingo Elías exports about 12,000 quintals of cotton annually from his own estates and some 28,000 more from the other haciendas. The port of Lomas, which was first opened by him a few years ago for exporting produce of the valley of Ica, is not down in [Robert] Fitzroy's chart. It is just to the south of the Mesa de Doña María, a high hill, off which is the rock of Los Infiernillos a league to the westward.

We were four days loading the *Jenny Lind* bound for London, during which time I dined on board. One night the curious old skipper and his wife persuaded me to stay later and play at whist with them, sending for a good-looking young mate to make a fourth. The bay was full of excellent fish, which we fried for breakfast, myriads of birds, and we saw some seals. One or two were swimming wearily to the Infiernillos. It is their cemetery, and their relations take them there to die.

On January 15 the *Jenny Lind* sailed and our party broke up. Mr. Ladd went back to Ica. He had been a pleasant companion and a good caterer. He told me he had a sister out here but no home for her, so she lives with some people at Nazca. He asked me to go and see her. I was to go along the seacoast for about forty miles to some huts called Santa Ana and then inland by San Javier to Nazca. For two-thirds of the way there was a line of cliffs about 450 feet high, some spurs of which project into the sea, forming little bays where herds of sea lions were sleeping.

Old Manuel, the Lomas fisherman, was my only companion. He managed to spear a large fish in the surf. At the same time I stripped and bathed, forgetting my former experience from the undertow. I was in danger of being dragged out but was saved by Manuel. Unfortunately for himself, the poor old chap is a murderer. In the middle of the night he often jumps up and runs screaming among the sand hills, thinking he is chased by devils and goblins.

At ten A.M. we arrived at the mouth of the river Ica, where the high cliffs cease. The sandy plain is covered by the same potash plant as at Villacuri. There were a few fishermen's huts here. We crossed the river easily and from this point a large bay sweeps round, ending in Point Nasca, a lofty and abrupt headland. The bay is called Puerto Caballos and was opened as a port for shipping cotton, but it is so much exposed that ships refused to go there. Point Nasca is a perpendicular cliff of sandstone much impregnated with salt, rising to a height of six hundred feet. From this point to the summit, another five hundred feet, there is an abrupt slope of loose sand. Halfway between the summit and the boiling surf the road, called *el mal paso* [the evil way], winds round for half a mile, being under three feet wide. Having passed this dangerous place, we had to ride for some miles along the beach and at three P.M. arrived at the bathing place of Santa Ana, a collection of huts built of canes and *huarango* poles at the mouth of the river of the same name.

In February Santa Ana often contains twenty or thirty families who come from Nazca and other valleys for the sea bathing; but when we arrived there were only two ladies, Doña Manuela Herrera and her mother, with whom I dined in the verandah of a long hut. The ladies were in great distress about two cows. They had strayed by a ravine to the top of the cliffs which rise up on each side of the river. They had tried to get down another way where the cliff becomes perpendicular and were standing there, unable from fright to move one way or the other. I volunteered to go to the rescue and managed by scrambling and climbing to reach the place, driving the cows up again from the danger and then down the ravine. The ladies were very grateful.

That night Doña Manuela's husband arrived and I was to go with him next morning to San Javier. He was a Gallego with red hair and moustache.

On the tableland near Santa Ana, at the foot of a lofty hill called Tunga, are several *huacas* and the ruins of stone houses where mummies and other relics have been found. It was probably an Inca fishing station.

After taking a warm farewell of poor old Manuel, Señor Herrera and I set out for the valley of San Javier in the morning of January the 16th. It was a ride of forty miles over a sandy desert of hills and dales. At last we went down a steep decline and reached the valley watered by the river Santa Ana, with its banks bordered by willows and *huarangos*. The whole of this extensive valley belongs to Don Domingo Elías and contains the three cotton haciendas of Santa Isabel de Lacras, San Javier, San José, and some smaller farms. Passing the small cotton estate of Coyungo, we rode through a wood of *huarangos* for some miles and by eight P.M. reached Lacras, where we passed the night. It is a new hacienda with a large courtyard, built five years ago under the direction of Mr. Ladd. Much cotton is grown on the estate, and there is a water mill for the machine to separate the seeds from the cotton and a press for packing the bales.

Two leagues farther up the valley is the large hacienda of San Javier, where there are extensive vineyards. The courtyard is surrounded by a colonnade with heavy round arches on two sides, three great wine presses on another, and a splendid church on the fourth. The carved woodwork of this church is very fine and the pictures are in richly carved gilt frames. At San Javier they make a very agreeable light wine and quantities of spirits. My travelling companion from Santa Ana, Don Pedro Herrera, was the *administrador*. The dinner at San Javier was made very interesting to me by the presence of an aged monk who had been at Montserrat in Catalonia at the time of the violent suppression [in 1837]. I had a long conversation with him.

The whole of this valley formerly belonged to the Jesuits, who introduced the Negro slaves and cultivated it most energetically. Their vineyards produced 70,000 arrobas of spirits annually, which they sold at $5 to $7 the arroba. The present price is $2. In the place of cotton they grew quantities of wheat, and near San Javier the ruins of their flour mill with the grindstones are still to be seen. They built the handsome churches of San Javier and San José in 1740 and a fine cloister at San Javier, where there are portraits of the generals of the order. After the suppression [in 1767] the Spanish government let the haciendas with bad results. The wheat disappeared and the vineyards were neglected. At last Don Domingo Elías bought them and restored their prosperity by attending to the vines and introducing cotton cultivation.

From San Javier I went on to the valley of Nazca. Passing by the ruins of an Inca pueblo, I came to the hacienda of San José, where there is a handsome church like that of San Javier. I dined there, continuing my journey in the afternoon. Further up the valley is the small village of Ingenio. Then there was a desert of twenty-seven miles to cross. The road, however, is hard and good and an hour after sunset I entered the vale of Nazca, taking up my abode in the village under the hospitable roof of the governor, Don Basilio Trigoso. My nicely furnished room opened on the courtyard. Beautiful creepers covered the walls, large pots of bright flowers rested in the forks of *huarango* posts, and cages with singing birds hung over them. A large arch led into this little paradise and faced the verandah opening on the living rooms. The Señora Trigoso and her family vied with Don Basilio in helping me and making me comfortable.

Nazca is a small and very quiet little town with one church and a suppressed convent. The church has been injured by an earthquake. But the valley in which it is situated, by the care of an ancient people—I think before the Inca conquest—has been converted into the most fertile and beautiful spot on the coast of Peru. It produces fruits and vegetables of excellent quality in abundance. The whole valley is covered with fertile haciendas. By an easy and gradual slope for six leagues the valley descends, widening until it attains a width of two leagues. Yet all that nature has given it is a small watercourse, almost always dry. The fertility is due to the skill and industry of the ancient inhabitants. Under their care an arid wilderness was converted into a smiling paradise, and so it has continued. This was effected by cutting deep trenches along the whole length of the valley and so far up the mountains that the present inhabitants do not know the positions of their origin. High up the valley the main trenches (*puquios*) appear, some four feet in height, roofed over and floored with stones and also with stone sides. Descending from the mountains, these covered channels separate into smaller conduits which ramify over the valley, supplying every hacienda with water all the year round and feeding the little streams which irrigate the fields and gardens. The larger *puquios* are many feet below the surface, and at intervals of about two hundred yards there are "eyes" (*ojos*) or manholes by which workmen can descend and clear away obstructions. By the time that all the channels have reached the end of the valley, nearly all the water has been used. At the termini of the *puquios* (called *bocas*) the tiny runlets of water flow out. I visited four of the *puquios,* descending into the *ojos* and wading some distance in the dark vault up to my knees.

There are fifteen vine haciendas and two cotton haciendas in the Nazca Valley, namely Cajuca (vine), owned by Don José Soto; Gobernadora (vine), owned by Don Fernando Ortíz; San Miguel (vine); Bisambra (vine); Achaco (vine); Pangaravi (vine); Cantayo (vine); Curbe (vine); Anglia (vine) and Ocaña (vine), owned by Don Basilio Trigoso; Belén (vine); Majoro (vine); Huachuca (vine and cotton); and Aja (vine and cotton). The two last belong to Don Agustín Muñoz. At Aja there is a water mill to work machinery for cleaning the cotton.

In the chain of mountains to the southeast of Nazca is a hill near which is the ancient gold mine of Cerro Blanco, which I went to see on January 20. Leaving Don Basilio's house under a scorching sun at eleven A.M., we rode along a road bordered on either side by fig trees and acacias, with bunches of grapes hanging over the vineyard walls. Then we entered a wood of *huarangos* and soon arrived at the foot of the hill, up which a steep and winding path led to the summit. I had left the Bdellium at San José for a good rest and been lent a horse belonging to the hacienda which could not face the steep ascent. So I left it in charge of a Negro and climbed up on foot. The way went over enormous blocks of rock, forming a very uneven staircase for two thousand feet. On either side were cacti, tall and gaunt. At last I reached the summit. Half a mile farther, over a rocky tract of country, brought me near the foot of the Cerro Blanco, where I found the mouth of one of the mines. Farther on was another larger mouth with two roofless stone huts near it and the ground strewn with old maize stalks and broken pottery. About fifty paces to the westward was a much deeper shaft running at an angle of thirty degrees to the southwest, and farther on were eight or ten smaller ones with their mouths strewn with bits of quartz and one piece of gold ore. At three hundred paces above the first mine I came to, I found the largest and principal shaft. At the entrance were two stone chambers with many bones of mules and *pisco* jars. In one chamber there was a recess in the wall and between the chambers was a high *huarango* post. The entrance to the mine was by a cavern about twelve feet high; at one side was a stone wall on which a wooden cross was placed. I went some way down until it became quite dark and then suddenly fell among the fallen stones until I was brought up all in the dark. In a great fright I scrambled up with some difficulty and reached the mouth. Near it I found a lump of quartz with veins of bright gold running through it. These mines have long been abandoned from want of capital, but they still contain gold and might repay anyone who undertook to work them. There is an extensive view from near the mines. The valley looks like a broad green river winding toward the sea, with deserts on either side, while behind rise the mountains one above the other to the clouds. Descending the hills once more, I found my horse and Negro. When I told the latter of my fall, he crossed himself. I returned to Nazca in time for a late dinner with the Trigosos.

In the evening I called on Miss Ladd and found her with a numerous and noisy family who, she said, was not sympathetic. The poor thing was moping and very homesick. I tried to cheer her up.

Next day I visited the hacienda of Anglia and some other *puquios*. I also examined the interesting ruins of an Inca pueblo on the opposite side of the valley. It is built in terraces up the side of the mountain, the houses with spacious rooms and niches in the walls, as at Herbay. In the centre, on a round hill, is a fortress with a semicircular wall in front and a high wall of defence at the back, its only approach being by a steep ramp from the pueblo. At the foot of the hill, corresponding with the semicircular wall, is a sort of outwork. The walk back to the town is very beautiful, along a lane bordered by orange, lemon, and fig trees.

On January 20, early in the morning, I left Nazca with great regret, in company with Don Basilio, and rode to his hacienda, where he gave me an excellent breakfast. I then went on to San Javier, where I found Don José Cintura, my travelling companion from Ica to Lomas. I took a long walk with him, examining the cotton plants, and in the evening I had coffee with the old *cura*, who talks Quechua.

I left San Javier early in the morning of the 21st, rode over an intervening desert, and came to the fertile and beautiful valley of Palpa. Entering the little town, I put up during the heat of the day at the hospitable dwelling of the governor, named Don José Mariano Tijero. He had been a soldier, was in most of the battles of the revolution, and told his stories well. He is now retired and looks after the family hacienda in the lovely vale of Palpa. It is called La Máquina, where he raises much cotton, cleans it with a machine, and sells it to Don Domingo Elías at $14 the quintal. A *puquio* works the machine and supplies the little town when the river is dry. Its origin is a thermal spring, which is warm in the morning but cool in the day and evening.

The valley of Palpa separates itself into two *quebradas* [ravines], those of Saramarca and Mollaque, both fertile and abounding in vineyards. There is an old gold mine on the hill between them and a very rich copper mine, which has just begun to be worked by Don Manuel Frías, the subprefect of Ica.

At five P.M., after an excellent dinner, I took leave of my kind host and, crossing the range of hills which separates the valleys of Palpa and Río Grande, entered the latter and crossed the river, which was very full. The whole of the Río Grande Valley belongs to Don Domingo Elías, who lets the vineyards and cotton plantations to small proprietors. A very lofty range of hills separates this valley from that of Santa Cruz, which is also covered with vineyards. My destination was the hacienda of Chimba, which I reached at sunset. After a rest of two hours I pushed on, entering the enormous desert, forty-two miles across, which separates the Santa Cruz Valley from Ocucaje. It is called the Pampa de Huayuri and there is not a single blade of vegetation in its whole extent. There was, however, a bright moon until three A.M. and by sunrise I reached the *huarango* wood near Ocucaje but did not stop and was at Ica by noon.

The Martínez family was very glad to see me again. I had my old comfortable room and stayed with them a week. I never knew people with whom one so quickly felt at home. On the 25th I went with them to the hacienda of San José, where there is a most luscious garden abounding in every kind of fruit. Don José Martínez was most kind. Knowing that I was interested in antiquities he took immense trouble in collecting some for me, and a large box of ancient pottery arrived safely in England. (Other friends at Ica contributed: Don Isidoro Elías sent one thing, Don Pedro Toledo another, Falconi another. One thing was valuable, a stone basin with serpents twined round it.) He also supplied articles of food for my journey across the Andes, with instructions about cooking them.

Don Juan de Dios Quintana had returned to Ica and exerted himself energetically to make all the best arrangements for my journey across the Andes and safe arrival at Ayacucho.

On the 27th Don Juan de Dios took me to a fiesta at a little village called Yauca near the foot of the mountains. We were accompanied by the rector of the College of San Luis Gonzaga at Ica and some ladies. The rector was a tall, stately person, with a florid complexion and aquiline nose, dressed in a long cassock, and with plenty of conversation.

The fiesta was very good fun, with a boy ringing two bells at once and lots of the usual crackers. Coming home we stopped at a little school by the roadside where the rector gave the best boy a real. I gathered from the conversation that the people here are very well off. The men get six reales a day and the boys two reales to a medio [half a peso] according to their size, while the women cook and work at home. Then, after working hours the men will go and cut *huarango* wood for fuel and send the children with it to town on donkeys, of which they have any quantity. The seeds of the *huarango*, deliciously sweet, make excellent food for horses, mules, and donkeys. Labourers frequently rent small patches of land at about one dollar a *fanegada*, where they raise *camotes*, beans, pumpkins, and watermelons, and the women go into market with them on donkeys in the mornings. Slaves get only their food unless they work on Sundays or feastdays, when they are paid at the same rate as free labourers.

I was to pass one night at Chavalina, the estate of Don Juan de Dios Quintana, at the foot of the mountains and near the road. He very good-naturedly went there on the 28th to see about my *arriero* and get everything ready for me. I was to follow next day, so I had one more day at Ica. The thermometer was eighty-eight to ninety degrees Fahrenheit. We went to the alameda and feasted on cooled fruit. At last I had to say farewell to these good, kind people. I was really sorry to leave the Martínez family and to think that I might never see them again, but of course it was inevitable. These partings are the worst of travelling.

Although Señor Quintana was doing everything, Doña Juana Martínez insisted on adding a spirit lamp, wine, bread, cheese, chocolate, *dulces*, spirits, and sugar. At last I left Ica on the morning of January the 29th. It is a ride of nine miles to Chavalina and I got there by ten A.M. The hacienda is situated at the entrance of the gorge by which the road to Ayacucho enters the mountains. The property extends on both sides, covered with vineyards. A short way up the gorge, Don Juan de Dios has recently formed another hacienda, named Mercedes after his dead wife, with large flower and fruit gardens. The estate of Chavalina formerly belonged to the Jesuits. It now produces some 20,000 arrobas of spirits a year, at $2 the arroba, nearly all of which is bought by Indians, who take it up into the sierra. Don Juan de Dios allows all his married slaves a piece of ground rent free, on which they grow vegetables and raise pigs and fowls, sending them into the market at Ica.

At Chavalina I was splendidly entertained, and a charming old housekeeper had another supply of provisions ready, beautifully packed. At dinner there were Don Juan de Dios, the housekeeper, myself, and the very nice little son and heir. Next day was a fiesta and there was a good deal of skylarking between young Quintana, aged about fourteen, and some slave girls. I took a walk with Don Juan de Dios, enjoying some interesting conversation. All was ready, the two mules saddled and loaded, and I started in the evening, my generous host riding about two leagues with me and then bidding me farewell. At Huamani, the first stage, I was joined by my guide and *arriero* named Agustín Carpio, a very respectable man and a very substantial person, who is employed in the lucrative business of conveying spirits up into the sierra. He rents three *fanegadas* of grazing land from Don Juan de Dios for $70 a year.

I was crossing the Andes by a little-frequented pass in the very worst time of the year, the height of the rainy season. I thought, however, that the scenery would probably be grander than at any other time.

Peru is divided into four longitudinal bands along its whole length: the coast, the *puna* or lofty and uninhabited part of the Andes, the sierra or inhabited part, and the *montaña* or eastern forests of the Amazonian basin. I had now completed the work I contemplated in the first region, that of the coast.

Chapter 8

Crossing the Andes

TO CROSS the Andes by an unfrequented route in the height of the rainy season was rather a formidable undertaking. At Huamani was the last vineyard. I and Agustín Carpio started at six A.M. on the 31st of January, 1853, passing for some miles up a valley covered with grazing farms well stocked with cattle, horses, and mules. We then entered an uninhabited ravine bounded on either side by steep mountains. Here I saw the first llamas, a flock of eight. The ravine ascended rapidly, with the river Ica dashing down it, bounded by willows, the graceful *schinus molle* [pepper tree] with its red berries, and a kind of laurel bush with a yellow flower called *chilca* (*baccharis scandens*). Emerging from the ravine, we commenced the ascent of a steep mountain by a zigzag road. During the great part of its length the ravine was bordered by stone terraces, eight or ten deep, becoming narrower as they ascended the mountain. Now unused, they showed that this wilderness was once a fertile and populous tract of country. Ascending the winding road, we were in a land of bright flowers, with a glorious view behind. Passing over the crest we came to a green and fertile valley abounding in alfalfa and vegetables. Here is the little sierra village of Tambillo and some terrace cultivation. The village is a

" . . . a girl was making a poncho of llama wool . . . in the same way as sword-mats are made on board ship."

collection of stone houses with red tiled roofs. The people all speak Quechua and dress in warm llama cloth. In the house where I stopped for luncheon, a girl was making a poncho of llama wool of various colours on a frame, in the same way as sword-mats are made on board ship.

On leaving Tambillo the water began to come down. The thick clouds descended to the earth charged with moisture, which was like a cold vapour bath. From January to March this commences between two and three P.M. and lasts until morning, swelling the rivers and sending down tons of water.

Through this we ascended up *cuesta* [hill] after *cuesta*, with precipices going down directly from the mule path, the bottoms of which were hidden by the mist and rendered awful by the roar of unseen waterfalls. At about six P.M. we reached the hamlet of Ayavi situated on the top of a hill covered with bright green herbage. It is thirty-six miles from Huamani. Here we stopped for the night in an uninhabited stone house. Having concocted pots of chocolate, I made up a bed of mule gear and went to sleep. There are about twenty inhabitants and a little church, but many of the houses are deserted and roofless. They have no windows nor chimneys and the cooking is done outside. In front of the houses there is usually a verandah. Two young women very civilly attended to us in the morning and cooked our breakfast.

We now entered the *puna* or lofty uninhabited part of the Andes. At six A.M. we started for the summit of the pass where Agustín said that there was a small natural cave for travellers to pass the night in. The road passes over broad slopes covered with *ichu* (coarse grass) rising one above the other and intersected by streams rushing down in every direction. Toward evening we reached the heights frequented by the vicuñas, most graceful and beautiful animals of a light fawn colour, with long slender necks, camel-like head, and very fine and silky fleece. There was also a number of animals between a very large hare and a squirrel, with short forelegs and bushy tails, called *viscacha*, a kind of partridge called *yuta*, and a loudly screaming plover. After riding for about twenty miles up a gradual ascent, we came to the region of snow called *ritisuyu*. Here, on a stony plateau, the road divides into two, one leading to Ayacucho, the other to the mining districts of Castrovirreyna and Huancavelica. A little farther on is the water-parting covered with snow. Thenceforward the water flows eastward to where

swell'd by a thousand streams impetuous hurled
From all the roaring Andes huge descends
The mighty Orellana. [James Thomson, "The Seasons"]

The sky was charged with thick mist and the snow was falling heavily while the roaring waters made a deafening noise. Perched about among the rocks were the *viscachas* sitting on their hind legs, while vicuñas were calmly resting on the snow with snow on their backs. The scene was wild and dismal. As the evening advanced we passed across a swampy plain and entered a narrow defile surrounded by perpendicular cliffs of black rock ending in peaks. This was where Agustín's cave is situated. We reached it just before dark. It consisted of an overhanging rock in the face of the cliff. But to our horror we found it full of water and streams dripping from the roof. The ground all round was covered with large tufts of grass a foot high charged with snow, making it uninviting to lie down. The snow was still falling and our matches had got wet. Agustín apologized by saying that he had never crossed in this season before and never thought it possible to be like what we saw and felt. In these very depressing circumstances Agustín Carpio, my guide, friend, and councillor, bowed his head on the mule's neck and announced that he was moribund. There was no help for it but to wait standing until daylight. I wrapped my poncho round and laid my head on the Bdellium's neck, who kept fairly quiet during the night. I experienced some difficulty in breathing from the great height, but nothing serious. Toward ten the thunder began to roar loudly around and below us with flashes of forked lightning.

As morning dawned it ceased to snow and things began to look more cheerful. The heavy mists gathered themselves together and rolled down the ravines, and at five A.M. we resumed our journey. Agustín began to recover his spirits. From the cave the road descends by a very steep declivity over slippery rocks. At length we completed the dangerous descent and came into the plain of Palmito Chico, with the river of the same name flowing down its centre. It was covered with excellent pasture where herds of cattle were grazing. It was bounded on one side by the snow-capped cordillera and on the other by a less elevated range with summits also covered with snow. The river was impassable and we had to take a round of two leagues to reach the *rumi chaca*, a natural stone bridge. Another league brought us to a shepherd's hut, the first habitation on the east side of the Andes, where we had breakfast. The little hut was round and about eight feet in diameter for the first two feet, and then a steep conical roof thatched with hay and supported in the centre by a maguey pole. The only inhabitant was a little boy, who was very civil and obliging. We next had to cross the river Palmito Grande which was also impassable, but the boy guided us to a little bridge his family had made. We then passed over a range covered with long grass and commenced another perilous descent, being very slippery from the water flowing over the rocks. Then we had to skirt along a precipice by a very narrow path. I was much pleased with the admirable presence of mind and surefootedness of my mules. At last a mass of projecting rock approached the other side of the abyss and here a few poles had been thrown across as a bridge. The torrent dashed over great masses of rock five hundred feet below, bordered by little bushes of a dark mournful green. The mules walked calmly across. On both sides the mountain rose quite perpendicular to a great height, with beautiful cascades coursing down in every direction. A league more of mountain road brought us to a narrow grassy plain surrounded by lofty peaks in which was situated a very much improved cave, La Cueva de San Luis, where we passed the night.

This cave is twelve feet deep, six high, and twenty broad, of red sandstone supporting a mass of conglomerate or pudding stone. Agustín contrived to supply a good repast and I was ravenous. But the night was bitterly cold and the morning was clear and frosty. We started at five A.M. and soon reached the crest of another steep descent where there was a high *apacheta* or heap of stones. Here the Indians throw over their burdens, pronounce the words "Apachicta muchhani," and each adds another stone. Having descended the *cuesta* we came to a ravine through which the river Hatunpampa dashes rapidly along. The road passes close to the edge of the torrent amidst beautiful scenery. Lofty mountains rise up on each side which are columniated, so to say, by the glitter of numerous waterfalls. The steep lower slopes (*talers*) were clothed with rich pasturage where sheep and cattle were grazing, with here and there a shepherd's hut.

At noon we reached the little hamlet of Hatun-sulla (Great Waterfall), which consists of a cluster of roofless stone huts with thorn trees (*tasta* [*stereoxylon patens*]) growing in the deserted rooms, and a little chapel. The only inhabitant was an old sacristan, who said that once a year people came to Hatun-sulla to celebrate a festival of the Virgin. Large flocks of llamas and alpacas were grazing around. After leaving Hatunsulla we came to a small hacienda at the foot of a lofty mountain where they are working the silver mine of Niñobamba. Down the same ravine, following the course of the river, the vegetation gradually became more abundant, wildflowers lined the sides of the road, and here and there were potato patches up the slopes of the mountains, which in other parts were covered with rich pasture. At five P.M. we came upon the Hatunpampa or great plain where cattle, sheep, llamas, and alpacas were grazing. Here the ravine opens to a width of three or four miles. We crossed the river with some difficulty and reached the grazing farm of Florida, where we were most hospitably received by the owner, named Medina. He was an interesting old person for he had served under Lord Cochrane and recounted his reminiscences to me. He gave us a delicious supper of *chupé* and bread and milk, and I had the first really comfortable sleep since leaving Chavalina. Next morning, after a good breakfast, we took leave of the hospitable old farmer, who positively refused to accept any remuneration.

Crossing a steep *cuesta* we left the Hatunpampa on the left and rode over a succession of grassy slopes until we reached and crossed a river called Ccica-machay (Grey Cave), with a little village of the same name. We then commenced the ascent of a lofty *cuesta,* so high, indeed, that gradually leaving a temperate climate we again entered the *puna* or cold region. At length, reaching the summit we entered upon the vast pampa of Cangallo, which extends for many leagues to the southward and is more than four leagues in width. A cold, bleak wind was blowing across the plain, which is covered with grass.

Here I met a traveler well muffled up, with his *arriero* and two cargo mules. He announced himself as Colonel Ormasa from Ayacucho going to Lima. When he heard who I was, he gave some directions to Agustín and then bade us farewell.

We then commenced the descent of a steep *cuesta* of slippery limestone, near the foot of which is the city of Ayacucho (formerly Huamanga). It appeared from this height a mass of red tiles nestling in a forest of fruit trees, which extended in different directions to the bases of the mountains. Directly opposite to us but beyond the city lay the broad grassy Pampa del Arco. The view is bounded in that direction by the heights of Condorcunca, at the base of which was fought the famous battle of Ayacucho in 1824. The name of the city was changed from Huamanga to Ayacucho to commemorate the battle. Descending the long and wearisome *cuesta*, we at once entered a temperate climate again. There was a long road lined with prickly pears and a background of fruit trees, then a ride down a charming avenue, and we were in the city. Agustín led me across the great square and under an archway into the courtyard of the prefect's house, where I was received with the greatest kindness and hospitality by the prefect, Don Manuel Tello y Cabrera, and his sisters.

The Bdellium and Cotham had done their arduous work extremely well and they would now have a month's rest, as Don Manuel lent me a roan horse during my stay.

Agustín Carpio was the best all-round *arriero* I ever met. He bade me farewell, being perfectly satisfied, and promised to report my safe arrival to Don Juan de Dios Quintana. I gave him $27 = £5.12. It was the 4th of February, 1853.

Chapter 9

Ayacucho

AYACUCHO IS 10,240 feet above the sea, at twelve degrees, fifty-nine minutes south latitude and seventy-three degrees, fifty-four minutes west longitude. In February the climate is equable and agreeable. In the morning it is usually clear with a blue sky. At about five P.M. heavy black clouds often come from over the mountains and there is an occasional thunderstorm. The temperature ranges from sixty-four to sixty-nine degrees Fahrenheit. The town is surrounded on three sides by mountains rising rather abruptly but with cultivation on their slopes wherever it is possible. To the east and north is the Pampa del Arco, a wide plain, and the mountains are ten miles away. The streets are at right angles, and in the centre is the *plaza mayor* or great square. On the south side is the cathedral and the *cabildo* or municipal building. The other three sides are occupied by private houses with red tiled roofs. In front of them are handsome arcades with stone pillars and circular arches, the ground floors being let as shops. The roof of the arcades makes a very wide balcony opening on the rooms, the roof extending for its width and supported by pillars. The southern part of the town was formerly separated by a deep ravine, but in 1804 Don Demetrio O'Higgins connected it by the *sutua chaca* and several other bridges and paved the streets. He was Spanish intendent from 1799 to 1810 [*sic*, 1812]. The alameda of Santa Clara was planted by his successor, Don Francisco de Paula Pruna, in 1812. There are several churches besides the cathedral; that of Santo Domingo is a very fine one with a space round it and trees. Huamanga was founded by Pizarro on April 1, 1539.[1]

The prefect and his people received me cordially and made me quite one of the family. He is a bachelor, with four sisters and their children living with him. They all became the greatest friends of mine and did everything they could think of to make my visit agreeable. I stayed a month in order to complete my training by mastering colloquial Quechua.

The grandfather of Don Manuel was Juan Basilio Tello, *subdelegado* [subdelegate] of the *partido* [district] of Andahuaylas in 1785. He represented the marquisate of Valdelirios, granted by Philip V in 1703. Don Manuel's uncle was Don Cypriano Santa Cruz, who owned the present family house at Ayacucho, and the brother of Don Cypriano was dean of the cathedral. One night a foundling was left at Don Cypriano's door. He adopted the child and it was the father of General Santa Cruz, so famous in Peruvian and Bolivian history.[2] From the dean the Tello family inherits the estate of Deanpampa near Ayacucho, and the large wheat hacienda of Totora was inherited from the marquisate. Don Manuel Tello's mother was a Cabrera. He himself was born in 1814. He was prefect of Ayacucho from 1844 to 1845 and from 1852 to 1854. He is of middle height, with auburn hair and reddish whiskers, a florid complexion, and good figure. He is amiable and kind-hearted, efficient as an administrator, and well informed. His house is not the prefecture, which is in another part of the town. He took me there and to the sittings of the superior court to see how business is transacted. He is still unmarried at forty but very happy with his sisters and their children round him.

Doña Josefa, called Chepita as a term of endearment, is the eldest sister, born in 1804, and is the widow of a Spanish officer. When [Ramón María] Narváez, the future Spanish prime minister, was serving here as a subaltern under the viceroy, [José de] La Serna, he proposed to Chepita and she refused him. She is a very charming old lady, with a mind steeped in folklore, and was my principal instructor in Quechua.[3]

Doña Mercedes, the second sister, is the widow of a colonel in the Spanish army whose horse was killed under him at Ayacucho. His name was Huguet. She is fairer and stouter than the others. Her four sons are Blas, an agreeable good-tempered youth of nineteen, studying for the law; Joaquín, I did not see as he was a subaltern quartered at Puno; José Antonio, a very good-looking lad, inclined to be studious; and Felipe

Neri, fair and sallow, with bright eyes, vivacious, and plenty to say about everything.

Doña Manuela, called Manunga, was the wife of Colonel Ormasa, whom I met on the Pampa de Cangallo. She has palpitations of the heart on account of her husband's absence and never leaves her bedroom. But she is clever and companionable, so we usually spent the evenings in her room, where we had tremendous suppers. I do not think there was much the matter with her. She was born in 1816 and had two children: Gertrudis, a very lively young lady of twelve, with red hair and fair complexion; and Estanislao, a very jolly little boy born in 1843.

Doña Micaela, called Miquita, is the youngest sister, born in 1825. She is the widow of General Juan Bautista Zubiaga, who was prefect of Ayacucho in 1840. His sister Francisca was the wife of the president, General [Agustín] Gamarra. The marriage of General Zubiaga and Micaela Tello took place when he was prefect. In 1842 General La Fuente sent him with troops to the valley of Jauja, where he encountered the forces of General Torrico, commanded by Colonel Lopera, at a place called Incahuasi. Zubiaga was mortally wounded. The news reached Ayacucho at night. Doña Micaela, without an hour's delay, mounted a mule and, heedless of the perils and dangers of the road in those unsettled times, arrived in time to receive her husband's last words, and he died in her arms. Doña Miquita has the remains of great beauty. She was my assistant instructor in Quechua. She had one precious child, Agustín, a charming and handsome boy of twelve, full of promise.

At the time of the revolution the Tello family was loyal and two had married Spaniards. They all fled to Cuzco and Bolívar confiscated the whole of the Tello property. Then the good deed of Don Cypriano Santa Cruz in adopting the foundling left at his door proved the salvation of the Tellos. By the intervention of General Santa Cruz, who had inherited a debt of gratitude to the family from his father, everything was restored to them.

A cousin of the family, Don Francisco Fernández, marquis of Moyobamba, who has a large estate on the road to Andahuaylas, often visits at Ayacucho and was there when I arrived. Our party was made up by old Colonel Mosol, the aide-de-camp, and a German boy they called Vendelin, obtained as a servant but who made himself quite one of the family, except that he messed with the other servants.

The wide balcony looked over the great square, where there was a very busy market in the mornings, the sellers sitting under shades made of wisps of straw on a pole, like huge umbrellas. This balcony was used as the general sitting-room. At one end was a door leading into a small but comfortable bedroom, which was assigned to me. The balcony led into

View of the Plaza of Ayacucho from the balcony of the house of Don Manuel Tello.

" . . . there was a very busy market in the mornings, the sellers sitting under shades made of wisps of straw on a pole, like huge umbrellas."

the dining room, beyond which was Don Manuel's room. On the side of the house in the street leading to the church of Santo Domingo was the long drawing room, very formal with chairs all along the walls and only used on state occasions. The other rooms looked on the courtyard and on the corral beyond, where my two mules were resting with unlimited alfalfa.

At breakfast and dinner we sat down thirteen: Don Manuel, the Señoras Chepita, Mercedes, and Miquita, Blas, José Antonio, and Felipe Huguet, Estanislao and Gertrudis Ormasa, Agustín Zubiaga, Colonel Mosol, the marquis of Moyobamba, and myself; but there were often guests. Our most frequent visitor was Jesusa Canseco, a niece of the dean, who lived opposite. She was very pretty, with a lovely complexion and blue eyes, but as mad as a March hare and up to anything. She was in and out incessantly. Another frequent guest was Doña Asunta (short for Asunción) Guzmán, and the fair Concita (short for Concepción) Espinosa came occasionally. What with Estanislao and Vendelin, Jesusa and Gertrudis, and others, there was generally a good deal of skylarking on the balcony.

In Lent there were "exercises" for a week at the nunnery of Santa

Clara, including self-inflicted penance with whips, and the nuns extended the hospitality of cells to any ladies that liked to come. All our ladies went, leaving us desolate. Presently Doña Miquita came back. She had forgotten her sins, which were written on a piece of paper. After a search they were found and she returned. Next Gertrudis bounded into the balcony, saying that when the whips were served out she thought it was time to come home. Don Manuel and Doña Manunga let us do what we liked, so Gertrudis proposed to have a dance in the sacred drawing room. We got Jesusa, Asunta, Concita, and some other girls to come, also a superior servant girl named Franciscacha, and a male friend of hers to play the piano. We kept it up until late, ending with a supper of assorted *dulces* in Manunga's bedroom. It was great fun but wrong in Lent, and the rest were shocked when they came back, especially Miquita about Franciscacha and the young man. Next morning I and young Zubiaga went to an early mass at Santo Domingo with Doña Miquita, and all was right again.

Don Manuel had a *quinta* [farm] just outside the town, with a summer house from which there was a lovely view and a garden full of all sorts of fruit trees. It was called Tartana. We went there on several afternoons and I made the acquaintance of two fruits that were new to me, one called *pacae* [*inga feuillei*]. It is a pod with a sweet woolly sort of juice between the seeds. The other is the *lúcuma* [*lucumo obovata*], not very good. When the Señora Chepita gave me fruit, she always said, "No hace daño" (It does no harm).

I had several rides on the roan with Don Manuel to Deanpampa and other properties of his. Although the climate of Ayacucho was charming, yet in some of the deep *quebradas* where one or two of these properties were, it was oppressively hot in the daytime and very cold at night.

The study of the Indians and their language was continued by me under the direction of Señora Chepita. The men are of course of the Quechua type, the women often handsome. The half-castes of Ayacucho are a good-looking race. In the morning the plaza presents an animated and picturesque appearance. It is covered with shades (*llantu*). A maguey pole is stuck in the ground supporting a framework circular roof, thatched with straw. Under these the women sit with their fruits, vegetables, cloth, and other goods spread out for sale, while numbers of people pass to and fro amidst the labyrinth of giant parasols.

Their dress is tasteful, displaying a variety of bright colours. Next [to] the skin the women wear a shift (*ucuncha*), over which is a shirt (*faldellín*) of crimson, blue, or purple woollen cloth. Round the shoulders is a mantle (*lliclla*) trimmed with ribbon or gold lace and fastened by a large pin of gold or silver in the shape of a spoon (*topu*), the poorer people using a small one of copper (*tipque*). On the head, folded in the shape of a triangle, is the *chuculli* of bright colours, sometimes used as a hood and called *reboso*. The bodice is of white cotton trimmed with red braid. Round the waist they wear an ornamental belt (*chumpi*). Many of them come to market from considerable distances, carrying their burdens on their backs in a coloured cloth (*ccepi*). Babies are carried in the same way. On the way they are employed in spinning cotton (*utcu*) or wool (*millma*) into thread (*ccaitu*), which they keep turning round and round by a handle (*heroru*). A great deal of coarse cloth is woven and dyed in the districts round Ayacucho. The men dress in a coarse blue woollen jacket and black breeches coming down to the knees, with sandals of untanned llama hide secured by strips of the same hide. They generally have a walking stick (*tauna*).

Their houses are built of unhewn stones, using damp earth as mortar, the frame of the roof being formed of beams of a sort of alder (*lambras* or *llampras*) and maguey poles and roofed with red tiles. The maguey or aloe is a most useful plant. The flower curving round the end of the long and elegant pole is called *hujuta*. The pole or stalk (*chuchau*) is a most useful timber for many purposes. The long pointed leaves (*pacpa*) are very strong and their fibres are made into ropes of different sizes, some of them into *sogas* or hawsers of which are made the bridges for crossing great rivers.

The food of the Indians consists of eggs, potatoes, onions, and yuccas, boiled in a pot called *manca*, and they also have bread which is very cheap, wheat abounding in the neighbourhood. Flour is sold at a dollar to a dollar and a half the *fanega* of six arrobas (one arroba = twenty-five pounds). They also use a great deal of maize (*sara*) and the young maize (*moti*). In their journeys parched maize is their only food, with coca [the leaf of the coca bush].

They drink a great deal of a fermented liquor made from the red berries of the *schinus molle*, as well as the *chicha* made from maize. They also have some knowledge of the medicinal use of certain herbs; for instance, they make a warm beverage of the scarlet salvia (*ccenti soncconan*) to cure coughs.

Their llamas come in droves with their Indian masters to buy corn in the town. They are able to bear great fatigue and to go without sustenance for a long time. But they are excessively self-willed, go just the pace they like, and will only carry three arrobas. If more is put on their backs, they sit down until it is taken off. The Indians never ill-treat them.

The Indians are very expert in working silver ornaments at the mines, where they make handsome utensils and beautiful filagree work. When anyone here has a spare lump of silver, he sends it to the mines to be worked up into a brooch or other ornament. They also show talent as sculptors. A very white alabaster abounds here which they make into perfectly formed figures and statuettes with only a knife and a little mallet.

Their artistic skill and knowledge of proportion are surprising. There is a quarry on the Pampa de Cangallo whence Don Manuel Tello has taken stone to make a new fountain in the plaza with a statue of liberty. It is being sculptured by two Indians without guide or assistance. The head and bust are already completed and are admirable. The pay of a day labourer here averages about three reales a day (nine shillings a week).

The Indians have been an oppressed race for three centuries. They have many songs but almost all are melancholy and despondent in their tone. The Señora Chepita obtained some for me which are sung to a guitar. The following song was given to me by the woman who kept the *chicha* shop at the corner of the Plaza de Santo Domingo:

> As the apple of my eye, O my beloved one,
> Thou are lost to me who dearly loved you.
> Mountains that divide the earth, have pity on me,
> Make the road to turn that I may go back.
> Heart of my beloved one, all the stones
> Stopping up the road hinder me.
> Flowing from village to village, the great river of Huarpa,
> Increased with tears for my love, hinders me.
> You, O cloud, whose water is like my eyes,
> Encompass me as I wait for my beloved.
> O falcon! lend me your wings that rising in the air
> I may then behold that which I wish for:
> When the heat is great or the rain falls,
> My beloved one resting, with a tree for shade.

Songs in alternate lines of Spanish and Quechua are also in vogue at Ayacucho and at Cuzco. One of these has a romantic story attached to it. A young priest in the province of Aymaraes was frantically in love with a beautiful maiden of the same place. Unable to restrain his love, yet fearing to break his vow, he went to Cuzco to try if absence would drive her from his memory. Soon after his departure, the poor maiden in climbing a steep path missed her footing and, falling down a precipice, was killed on the spot. She was buried in the little church and shortly afterwards her priestly lover, unable longer to absent himself, returned. On hearing of the maiden's mournful death, he could no longer restrain his deep unchanging love. Rushing into the church, with sacrilegious hands he tore the corpse from its shroud and, embracing it tenderly as when living, he broke forth impromptu into a wild song [that ended in a request for death]. It is said that the request was complied with. The unfortunate youth died with the beloved but ghastly form in his arms and was borne away to hell by three devils.

The Señora Chepita continued to instruct me and often had Indians in to practice talking or to hear their songs and traditions. Melancholy seemed to pervade their thoughts. Intelligent, artistic, industrious, they were despondent. Only the children ever played at games. A sort of hopscotch was the favourite, which they called *cachorro*. Estanislao and Vendelin used to play at it in the corral. It was rather different from what the small boys used to play at Cheam.

But the time was approaching for resuming my journey to Cuzco. March 7 was the day fixed. No words can express what I felt. They were like near relations. One day a visitor was announced. It was the great Chilean preacher, Dr. Don Francisco de Paula Taforo. He was banished for taking part in the recent very sanguinary insurrection against [Manuel] Bulnes in Chile. Dr. Taforo was sitting in the drawing room in state. For the last fortnight he had been arousing the enthusiasm of the religious world in Ayacucho by his brilliant oratory. He came to propose that we should travel together as far as Cuzco. He was a tall man with a slight figure and a very distinguished air, in a cassock, long cloak, and biretta. His face was pale, with a thin, slightly aquiline nose, high fore-head, and penetrating eyes, but with a bright, kindly expression. We at once took a strong liking for each other. He could not start with me owing to religious engagements, but he was to overtake me at Andahuaylas.

The Bdellium and Cotham were fat and well-rested. At last the sad day arrived. I wanted to take Vendelin with me but Estanislao could not part with him. All was ready. My happy month was at an end. I went into the Señora Manunga's room and she embraced me with tears, saying "Ah, ¡Don Clemente! Vienes darme pena" [You have come to make me sad]. The Señoras Chepita, Mercedes, and Miquita were a little less demon-strative in their farewells but equally sincere. The boys and Gertrudis crowded round me with warm and cordial wishes. Gertrudis and Esta-nislao cried. I was quite overcome and perfectly miserable. Don Manuel and Blas Huguet rode with me as far as Deanpampa. There we parted, waving our hats until we lost sight of each other by a turn of the road.

Chapter 10

Excursions from Ayacucho

I MADE three excursions from Ayacucho, one to Huanta in hopes of seeing Iquichano Indians, who interested me, one to the battlefield of Ayacucho, and one to the battlefield of Chupas. On February the 10th I started to visit Huanta, twenty miles to the northward, mounted on a splendid mule belonging to Don Manuel. Crossing the Pampa del Arco the road passes up and down three *quebradas* or ravines and then commences the descent of a steep and very long *cuesta,* at the foot of which winds the river Pongora in a warm tropical valley covered with fields of maize and wheat, with haciendas and mills on the banks of the river. On the other side of the valley is the village of Pacaicasa, surrounded by prickly pears, fig trees, *lucuma* and *pacae* trees. Ascending another steep and slippery *cuesta,* we came upon a large plain in which is the Hacienda Vega belonging to Don Remijirio Jauregui, subprefect of Huanta. The house is in the midst of wheat and maize fields. After two miles more of very bad road we reached the bottom of a deep ravine where a stone bridge of one arch spans a torrent. Arriving at the crest of a hill on the other side, we entered the little village of Macachacra and came in sight of Huanta, situated in a fertile plain and bounded to the east by lofty and snow-clad mountains. The road was lined with willows and *schinus molle*, cacti of different kinds, maguey, and numbers of flowers.

Arriving at Huanta, I was hospitably received by the subprefect and the Señora Jauregui. They gave me an excellent supper and comfortable bedroom. The señora sat in a gorgeous armchair. The back was in three stripes, red, white, and red satin, the Peruvian colours.

Huanta is a small town consisting of a plaza with streets leading from it and surrounded by fruit gardens. To the eastward the lofty mountains of Iquicha rise up, at first in cultivated slopes but ending in perpendicular cliffs. Behind them is the wild country of the Iquichanos, consisting of almost inaccessible fastnesses. The Iquichanos were loyal and fought furiously for the Spanish cause and against the revolution. In 1828 they advanced on Ayacucho, proclaiming Fernando VII, but were defeated on the Pampa del Arco by the citizens and the Morochuco Indians, who were equally keen for the revolution. The Iquichanos now come into Huanta to buy cotton and sell their wool and vegetables. I saw several of them in the plaza. They were distinguished by an upright gait, independent air, and regular features. They wore a peculiar *montera* or cap. I returned to Ayacucho on February the 11th.

On the 13th I started to examine the battlefield of Ayacucho, accompanied by Colonel Don Antonio Mosol, who himself served in the battle. Passing across the Pampa del Arco, we descended into the deep valley of Pongora and passed several haciendas. That of Don Manuel, called Totora, is surrounded by fig trees, vines, and alfalfa. Further on are those of Glorieta and Santo Domingo, with corn mills over the river, and on the hills above wheat is extensively cultivated. Crossing the Pongora, we ascended a long *cuesta* which led to an elevated plain covered in many places with bushes called *chilca*. A ride of five miles brought us to the little village of Quinua, surrounded by quantities of *lambras* trees, a sort of alder, with fields of vegetables. After supper, a very excellent one provided under the superintendence of Doña Mercedes, we made up beds with our mule gear in the verandah of the *cura*'s house, who was absent; but it was bitterly cold. Quinua is at least six hundred feet higher than Ayacucho.

Early next morning I started with the colonel to explore the battlefield, which is not more than a quarter of a mile from the village.

The Spanish army under the viceroy, La Serna, started from Cuzco, advancing to meet the rebel force of Colombians and Peruvians under General [Antonio José de] Sucre. For some time they had been marching in parallel lines. On December 6, 1824, the royalists occupied Quinua. Both Huamanga and Huanta were in their hands and the rebels had not a foot of ground except what they actually stood upon. They numbered about seven thousand men.

"They were distinguished by an upright gait, independent air, and regular features."

The range of mountains called Condorcunca (Condor's Neck) is very steep and rises about two thousand feet above the plateau of Ayacucho, which slopes down toward Quinua. It is of small extent, about a mile wide, bounded to the south by the deep and almost perpendicular ravine of Hatun-huayccu and to the north by the much less deep and wider depression of Venda-mayu, down which flows a stream bordered by *lambras* trees. After running east and west for a mile, the Venda-mayu turns and divides Quinua from the battlefield. In the corner, where the ravine of Venda-mayu descends from the heights of Condorcunca, is the place called Ayacucho (Corner of the Dead), where an Inca army totally defeated the ancient inhabitants of this part of the country called Pocras. Here there is an old ruined wall called Pucahuasi.

The Spanish army evacuated Quinua and made a long march by Pacaicasa, Vega, and Huamangilla, finally occupying a position high up on the heights of Condorcunca on the 8th of December. They were about eleven thousand strong, under the viceroy in person who was with the division of [Alejandro González] Villalobos, and had eleven pieces of artillery. The spot was called Chicchi-cancha, close to the ravine of Hatun-huayccu. General [José de] Canterac, a Frenchman in the Spanish service, was in the centre with two divisions, and in the right wing, at the head of the ravine of Venda-mayu, was the brave but cruel General [Jerónimo] Valdés.

The rebel army occupied Quinua, and on the 7th General Sucre established his headquarters at the ruined chapel of San Cristóbal, on the field. General [Jacinto] Lara, a Colombian, with three Colombian battalions formed his centre. His left, near the Venda-mayu, was composed of five battalions of Peruvian infantry commanded by General [José de] La Mar, and the whole of the cavalry (two Peruvian and two Colombian squadrons) under Miller, with one eight-pounder field piece. The right wing facing the viceroy consisted of four Colombian battalions under General [José María] Córdoba, a young man aged twenty-six, with his right flank resting on Hatun-huayccu. It was a model battlefield, almost a *champ clos*. Córdoba faced the viceroy, Lara was opposite to Canterac, and the Peruvians under La Mar were opposed to Valdés.

Sucre held a council of war in which it was unanimously resolved to fight on the morrow as the rebels had no provisions and their ammunition was running very low; so hungry indeed were they that the sign and countersign were *pan y queso* (bread and cheese). At about midnight, reckless young Córdoba marched across the plain with two hundred men, silently climbed the steep ascent, and fired a volley into the royalist watch fires; then retreated at the double. This caused the death, among others, of the Spanish Brigadier Palomares, who was sleeping. There is now a small cross on the spot where he died.

Early in the morning the two armies beat to arms. The viceroy with the division of Villalobos came down from the heights and took up a position on the field, with the field guns on his left flank. Valdés, with the object of taking the rebels in the rear while the viceroy and Canterac attacked them in front, advanced down the ravine of Venda-mayu. He had forced his way almost to the rear of the chapel of San Cristóbal with his division of infantry and the cavalry regiment of San Carlos when he was met by the Peruvian division of La Mar, and a desperate struggle ensued. But La Mar was reinforced by Lara's division, and Miller, with the whole rebel cavalry, charged Valdés in the rear, who was overpowered and surrendered with all his forces. Meanwhile Córdoba advanced across the plateau with four battalions, muskets on their shoulders and reserving fire to the last moment. The Spanish artillery fired a few volleys but with too much elevation, and the rebels dashed forward and captured the guns after a short but desperate encounter with the division of Villalobos. The viceroy was preparing to go to the aid of Valdés with his cavalry. Not having room to charge, however, he was assailed by Córdoba's infantry and his squadrons were thrown into confusion. The viceroy fired at a rebel sergeant, who returned the compliment, wounding La Serna on the nose, and was about to run him through when he cried out, "Hold, I am the viceroy!" and was taken prisoner. He afterwards gave the sergeant $100 for sparing his life.

During the whole action, Canterac with the royalist centre never descended the heights, and when he saw the viceroy taken prisoner he hoisted the white flag and came down to capitulate. Canterac's inaction lost the battle. Besides the viceroy, Valdés, Villalobos, and Canterac, the rebels took eleven generals and a proportional number of other officers, including the subaltern Narváez [*sic*], afterwards so famous in Spanish history, with an immense quantity of arms, ammunition, horses, and eleven field guns. A capitulation was signed on the field of battle by which the Spanish officers and all the men who wished it were to be sent to Spain at the expense of the Peruvian government. During the night after the battle there was a tremendous storm of thunder and lightning.

The victors now ceased to be rebels and became the rulers of the country. Much gratitude was felt for the heroes of the battle. They ruled the country for forty years and distracted it by civil wars among themselves. The executive was practically independent of the legislature and corruption and tyranny were the result. The ordeal was inevitable but military ascendancy at length ceased. Among the officers at the battle of Ayacucho were:

Rank at the time	Name	Future Position
General	La Mar	president
General of Brigade	Gamarra	twice president
Adjutant General	Castilla	twice president
Aide-de-Camp to La Mar	Nieto	a prominent general
Lieutenant [*sic*, Captain]	Salaverry	supreme chief
Second Lieutenant	Pezet	president
Sub-Lieutenant	Torrico	supreme chief
Colonel	Bermúdez	supreme chief
Second Lieutenant	Vivanco	supreme director
Captain	San Román	president
Lieutenant	Espinosa	author
Cadet	Deustua	general

After walking over every part of the field with my admirable guide, we returned to Quinua for breakfast and got back to dinner by four P.M. My sole authority for the incidents of the battle was Colonel Mosol, whose memory was perfect and whose mind was quite clear from bias or partiality. That evening the campaign of Ayacucho was the chief topic of conversation in the Señora Manunga's room, all but Felipe Huguet holding that the royalists would have won but for the inaction of Canterac.

On the 26th of February I started, with young José Antonio Huguet, to visit the battlefield of Chupas, fought between Almagro the lad and the Licentiate Vaca de Castro on September 16, 1542. Riding up the steep road by which I had entered Ayacucho and halfway up the *cuesta* above it, we turned abruptly to the left and, passing over several spurs, descended into the steep ravine of Lambrashuayco, through which runs the stream of the same name bordered with *lambras* trees. It supplies Ayacucho with water. On the opposite side of the ravine and above it is the spur of Chupas. It slopes down from the heights of Atunhuana, beyond which is the great plain of Cangallo. It is high above Ayacucho. The pampa or plateau is bounded on one side by the ravine of Lambrashuayco and on the other by a smaller ravine, on the other side of which is the wheat hacienda of Cochabamba belonging to Don Manuel Tello. A great part of its northwest side is covered with wheat, with a few huts scattered here and there amidst thickets of broom. At the foot of the heights is the wheat hacienda of an old gentleman whose acquaintance I had made at Ayacucho, usually known as Cojo (Lame) Arias. On the southeast side is an open plain with several inequalities and covered with grass. At this season it is rather swampy. Nearer the heights are some hills with sides forming declivities and gullies between them. This, I think, was the battlefield.

When Pizarro was assassinated [in 1541], the Licentiate Vaca de Castro was on the way to Peru to investigate and report upon the state of affairs. The friends of Almagro, after the perpetration of the crime, had resolved to make for Cuzco, taking young Almagro with them. This young man was in his twentieth year and was always called *el mozo* (the lad). His mother was Ana Martínez of Panama, where the boy was born. She was not married to Almagro but the offspring was legitimatized in 1529. The boy came to Peru in 1535 with Francisco Martín de Alcántara, Pizarro's half-brother. He was sent to Cuzco with Juan de Rada to follow his father into Chile. Before the death of his father at Cuzco, Almagro the lad was taken to Lima by Alonso de Alvarado, and at first Pizarro had him to live in his own house but afterwards sent him away because his father's friends came to see him. On Pizarro's death, those of the Almagro party left Lima, taking the lad with them and proclaiming him as his father's successor as they marched to Cuzco.

Several leading men remained loyal, chief among them being Pedro Alvarez Holguín, who had returned from exploring Carabaya. He was joined by Gómez de Tordoya and others, but they were not strong enough to oppose the march of Almagro the lad. They managed to pass him and went to join Vaca de Castro. With them were Garcilaso de la Vega, Pedro Hinojosa, and Diego Centeno.

Young Almagro left Lima with 817 well-armed men, 280 being cavalry, and 5 guns. Juan de Rada, the leader of the assassins, was old and ill. He died at Jauja. Juan Tello commanded the cavalry; Diego de Hoces, Martín Cote, and Cárdenas the infantry; Pedro de Candía the artillery. They reached Cuzco and tried to negotiate, but Vaca de Castro would listen to nothing less than unconditional surrender. His advance was continued, Holguín being appointed second-in-command. At Jauja he mustered seven hundred men with three or four falconets and by forced marches he reached Huamanga when Almagro was at Vilcashuamán.

Almagro had marched out of Cuzco to meet the royal governor, who refused all terms with him. He had sixteen pieces of artillery commanded by Pedro de Candía, one of those who crossed the line at the isle of Gallo with Pizarro.[1] He had five hundred of his father's veterans, two hundred mounted and many in complete mail. He had help and guides from the Incas, Manco and Paullu. He formed his cavalry into two squadrons, one led by himself and [Juan] Balsa, the other by his chief of staff, Pedro de Oñate, with Diego Méndez and Saucedo. The infantry was led by Juan Tello de Sotomayor, Juan de Oña, Martín Bilbao, and Diego de Hojeda. Cote was in command of the arquebusiers, and with the standard were Juan Fernández de Angulo, Baltazar de Castilla, Juan Ortíz de Zárate, Pantoja, and Juan de la Reynaga, with 550 good soldiers under them.

Advancing from Vilcashuamán by a mountainous route through Cangallo, guided by Indians of the Inca, Almagro the lad intended to attack Vaca de Castro by a descent from the heights above Huamanga. This was a well-conceived plan, but the enemy got wind of it and Vaca de Castro led his whole force up at Chupas. Soon the contending armies came in sight. Both leaders formed their cavalry on the wings, that arm of the royalists being led by Holguín, Gómez de Alvarado, Garcilaso de la Vega, and Pedro González de Campo-redondo. Cristóbal de Barrientos carried the royal standard, with a guard under Alonso de Alvarado. The royal infantry in the centre was led by Juan Vélez de Vergara.[2] Nuño de Castro commanded the reserves. Cruel old Francisco de Carvajal was sergeant major. The whole royal force numbered 800, 170 being arquebusiers. Vaca de Castro had with him twenty cavalry to help where needful, with Lorenzo de Aldana, Gómez de Rojas, Diego de Agüero, and others.

The battle was desperately contested and was long doubtful. Holguín was killed early in the day and Gómez de Tordoya was mortally wounded. Vaca de Castro rode a black horse and wore a rich surcoat with the habit and emblems of Santiago over his armour. Almagro the lad formed his army along the crest of a rising ground to await an attack, his artillery opening fire with some effect as the enemy approached. Carvajal then undertook to lead the troops by a circuitous route round the declivities of some hills, protected by rising ground until quite close. When they again came in sight, the artillery opened on them with fatal effect at first, but afterwards with too much elevation. Young Almagro suspected treachery and that this was done on purpose. He ran Pedro de Candía through the body and pointed the guns himself, shooting down several of the royalist cavalry. Some other shots mowed down the infantry. The royalist forces were ordered to charge.

The lad then made a fatal mistake. Instead of standing his ground where he was, he came down to meet his enemies. The shock took place on the plain and there was a desperate fight. The royalists began to fall back. Carvajal rallied them and gallantly led a charge of infantry on the guns, which he captured.

It was now dusk. The lad attacked Alonso de Alvarado, who was on the right, and drove him back, crying, "Take but kill not." At that moment Vaca de Castro came up with his reserves and the tide turned. Many fell, but Almagro and his gallant men were borne back. As night came on, the rout was complete, the heroic lad being carried off by the rush. It was nine P.M.

The dead were buried in long trenches. The body of Holguín was brought to the church of San Cristóbal at Huamanga. Out of Almagro's 850 men, it is said that 700 were killed. The victors lost 350. The lad escaped to Cuzco.

There was a commission at Huamanga to try the prisoners under the licentiate Antonio de la Gama. The number condemned to death was forty, and of these thirty were beheaded.

Almagro the lad was evidently a youth of considerable ability and dauntless courage. He was captured at Cuzco and beheaded. His body was buried by the side of that of his father in the church of La Merced.

I went over every part of the ground, making out the positions, and then had a fairly decent luncheon with Don Bonifacio, the *administrador* of the hacienda. Returning to Ayacucho in the evening, we met Cojo Arias in the alameda and had some conversation with him. He said something about bones and a spear having been found on his estate. He also told me that Alonso de Alvarado had been engaged in the conquest of Chachapoyas and brought some Chachapoyans with him. Their services in the battle obtained for them a grant of land and exemption from tribute. They founded the village of Chiara near Chupas.

We got back to Ayacucho in time for a late dinner and had the usual conversation about our day's experiences in the Señora Manunga's room.

Chapter 11

Ayacucho to Cuzco

I LEFT Ayacucho on the 7th of March riding the Cotham, the Bdellium carrying the cargo, attended by a cavalry soldier who was to take me as far as Andahuaylas and to cook when necessary. I was exceedingly down-hearted at leaving my friends and much depressed. Passing by the pantheon, the road leads down a deep ravine full of the most beautiful wildflowers. Here there are water mills for grinding corn and haciendas surrounded by fruit gardens, with wheat and barley fields.

At five P.M. I reached the humble little post-house of Pucavilca, where I passed the night. Early next morning we again started over the same sort of country, until at noon we arrived at the farmhouse of Matará, where I stopped for luncheon. The whole extent of country is capable of cultivation and might sustain more than ten times the present population. In a large patch of land near Matará were twelve ploughs of the very simplest construction at work with bullocks at the same time.

Here I made a mistake through ignorance. The very interesting and important ruins of Vilcashuamán, in the province of Cangallo, might have been reached from Matará, but it was not until afterwards that I knew of their importance.

Leaving Matará and passing through a little copse of thorn trees, we commenced the ascent of the Condorcunca range, up a most trying path for the mules. The descent was worse and more steep. At last we reached the little village of Ocros at six P.M. Surrounded by high mountains, the vicinity is still covered with maize and bean fields, each having a hut in one corner while large patches of wheat extend up the steep mountains, apparently with such a gradient that it becomes difficult to understand how the ploughing bullocks can have found foothold.

Next morning we left this interesting little village and continued the descent down into the profound valley through which flows the great river Pampas to join the Apurímac. Gradually leaving the temperate regions of the sierra, in two hours we were in a tropical valley covered with close underwood and tall aloes. There were flocks of green parrots and many glittering hummingbirds fluttering about and sucking honey from the flowers. The mountains we had descended rose in frowning majesty, in one place quite perpendicular from the valley, and through its centre flowed the great river. In a narrow place about twenty yards wide, a bridge of *sogas,* or ropes made of the twisted fibres of the maguey, had been thown across the chasm. Six *sogas,* each about a foot in diameter, are stretched over the river and set up on the other side by a windlass. Across these hawsers other smaller ropes are secured and covered with matting, which forms the bridge. It is considerably lower in the centre than at the ends and it vibrated up and down a good deal as we passed over it. This bridge has to be renewed several times in the year.

After riding down the valley of the Pampas for two leagues, we began the ascent of the lofty *cuesta* of Bombón, which is more than two leagues long and covered with *lambras* and *molle,* while the rugged peaks of the ridge rise up in rocky pinnacles on either side of the road. On the crest and beyond, it was a more temperate climate. In the lowest part is a sugarcane hacienda belonging to the Tello family. In this valley is the pretty little village of Chincheros, where I passed the night under the very hospitable roof of the governor. The family was very anxious about my travelling so far away from home and showed much sympathy for my loneliness. The wife as good as asked me if "my mother knew I was out." We sat long, talking outside the house facing the fine old tree in the centre of the plaza.

Next morning, passing over an elevated and at this season very swampy plain covered with herds of cattle, we reached the post-house of Uripa, in another well-peopled valley, with fields of maize, potatoes, and beans and the sides of the hills sown with wheat. A little brook runs through the centre of the vale of Uripa and the summits of the surrounding mountains are clothed with trees. Leaving this lovely and peaceful scene, we entered a narrow gorge between steep and grassy mountains, ending in irregular peaks, through which a noisy torrent was babbling over the masses of rock which were strewn along its bed. The road was lined with a profusion of trees and flowers. Here we stopped to have luncheon in a lovely spot. At about noon we proceeded and began the ascent of a long *cuesta*, leading to a wide and elevated plain covered with long grass, where a flock of vicuñas was feeding in the distance. As we came to the end of this vast pampa, a thunderstorm burst over the opposite range of mountains. The storm, which pealed forth in loud and threatening tones and sent out brilliant forked lightning, passed rapidly away to the northwest without touching us. At six P.M. we reached the little post-house of Moyobamba, where I dined and passed a fairly comfortable night.

Next morning, descending a narrow but very picturesque ravine with a torrent dashing down a rocky bed many feet below us, we turned the point of a high cliff and came in sight of the lovely valley of Andahuaylas. The road took us across the river of the same name, through the village of Talavera, to Andahuaylas, where I was hospitably received by the subprefect, Don José María Hermosa. The house is on the side of a hill overlooking the town. I had a large and very comfortable room with a lovely view of the valley. The dining room was under a shed in the back yard, quite open on two sides. The subprefect said that being in the open air, there was no smell of dinner. There were several guests, and the handsomest and most upright Indian women I had yet seen came to sell fruit. Señor Hermosa's wife was dead but he had four of the quaintest little children, dressed in the most old-fashioned way, who quite took possession of me—Miquita, Nicanor, Adelaida, and Angelita. I suspect my room was in ordinary times the dining room and that it had been cleared out and fitted with a bed for me. The children delicately hinted as much.

The vale of Andahuaylas is the most beautiful I have yet seen in the sierra. Running nearly east and west, it contains three small towns about a league distant from each other, called Talavera, Andahuaylas, and San Gerónimo. Through its centre runs the little river, lined on either side by very tall poplars. I measured one [and calculated it was] ninety-two feet. Hitherto I have called them willows, but they must be poplars. Every here and there large fruit gardens come down to the riverbanks. Every part of the valley is carefully cultivated, with maize, potatoes, and all kinds of vegetables, and the sides of the hills are covered with maize crops. Andahuaylas, one hundred miles from Ayacucho by the road, consists of a plaza, with a handsome stone church and a fountain, and with a few streets leading from it.

In the evening of March 11, to my astonishment, I received a note from Dr. Taforo, who had reached Talavera, and the next day he was the guest of a nice family in the plaza of Andahuaylas. In the evening of the 12th he preached a sermon before an immense concourse of people on the Lord's

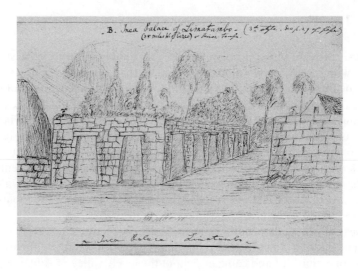

B. Inca Palace of Limatambo — (_or miles W. of Cuzco_) _or Huiac Tampu._

Inca Palace. Limatambo.

" . . . only two walls and the wall of a wide terrace on which the palace was built are still remaining." (See p. 84.)

Prayer, explaining and enlarging on its seven petitions with great fervour and eloquence. With his tall, slight figure in a tight black satin cassock, pale but very handsome face, and graceful declamation, he looked the embodiment of a missionary saint. He was always the same to everybody and treated the poorest Indian with the same courtesy and consideration as he would show to the highest in the land. When he left the church, crowds of people flocked round him to kiss his hand or touch the hem of his garment.

Next day I had to bid farewell to Señor Hermosa and my little friends and joined company with Dr. Taforo. In the afternoon we went on to San Gerónimo, attended on horseback by all the principal people of Andahuaylas, and were hospitably received in the house of the vicar. He was a priest of some learning and had a considerable library, including folios of the early Fathers. But he was bursting with fat and in his shirt sleeves.

On March 14 we continued our journey to Cuzco, the whole of our march from this point being a sort of triumphal procession, messengers being sent before to announce our approach. It was a great thing for me to have a well-informed man like Taforo to talk to on the road.

Leaving San Gerónimo we passed over an elevated plain and, entering the rich and fertile vale of Argama, had breakfast at the post-house. The road then leads over a _cuesta_ covered with flowers and shrubs which divides the vales of Argama and Pincos. The latter is more profound and in one part contains several sugar haciendas. Leaving the vale of Pincos, we had to skirt for two leagues along the sides of the mountains in the midst of magnificent scenery. There is a small plateau beyond, on which is situated the ancient fortress of Curamba. Though small it has some interest connected with Inca history, having been originally a stronghold of the Chancas. Curamba is a square fort of solid masonry in three terraces, one above the other, the wall of the outer terrace being thirty feet on each side. The upper terrace is approached by a ramp from the plain, with a slope sufficient to enable a mule to ride up to the summit. There are extensive ruins near the fort, the whole overgrown with bushes. The fort is now surmounted by a wooden cross.

From Curamba we descended a long *cuesta* to the village of Huancarama, where we were hospitably received in the house of a widow with three daughters. They were in great distress owing to the disappearance of the husband and father. He was supposed to have fallen down some precipice. After supper we were put to sleep in a large room, Taforo's bed in one corner and mine in another. In the dead of night I was awakened by a noise. There was a bright moon and I saw a figure—I thought it was in a poncho—and a ghastly face gliding across the room. Taforo was sitting up with his hand pointed to it and saying some exorcism and the office for the dead in a loud voice. I promptly put my head under the bedclothes. On my asking about it next morning, he said that the widow had complained of an apparition in that room and that he had decided to sleep there. He added, "It will not come again." I thought to myself that he might at least have given me the choice of the verandah.

Huancarama is situated in a fertile and thickly populated valley surrounded by lofty mountains. The church, which is half unroofed and in a very neglected state, to my surprise still possesses an altar covered with plates of silver beautifully worked. We had an early mass. The thermometer was fifty-five degrees Fahrenheit at ten P.M. and sixty-two at ten A.M.

After mass, on the 15th of March, we set out accompanied by the *cura* and five or six others on horseback, while numbers of girls lined the road on each side and covered us with flowers. Having completed the ascent of a lofty *cuesta*, we came in sight of the extensive and beautiful valley of Abancay, covered in its whole length with fields of sugarcane, which gave it a rich and warm colouring. It is lined on either side by ranges of very steep mountains, with their summits running up into peaks and covered with foliage. Far up the valley, surrounded by trees, we could make out the town of Abancay. Descending a long and stony *cuesta* which brought us from a temperate to a tropical climate, we stopped at the sugar hacienda of Carhuacarhua and were refreshed by some delicious lemonade. The cane is smaller and not as good as that on the coast and the mill is worked by water. The machinery is very simple, the wheels and even the cogs by which one is connected with another being of wood.

Passing down the valley by several sugar haciendas, each including fruit gardens, we arrived at the point where the important river of Pacha-chaca crosses the valley to join the Apurímac. At the bottom of a deep ravine it flows rapidly but silently onwards and is spanned by a stone bridge of one arch, at a great height above the water, built in Spanish times. Crossing the Pachachaca we reached Abancay after dark and were very hospitably received by the subprefect, Don Paulino Mendoza, a nephew of the bishop of Cuzco. We remained during the 16th at Abancay. It is a pretty little town with a stone church and a few streets leading from it, surrounded by fruit and vegetable gardens, with many tall and vener-able trees. To the southwest is a flowery ravine, at the bottom of which the river Abancay flows to join the Pachachaca. On the opposite side a range of mountains rises abruptly to an immense height so that their sum-mits are within the snow line. It is here that the varied products of a coun-try doubly blessed by nature may be seen at a glance. Just below the sum-mits herds of cattle and flocks of sheep were feeding on rich pasture. Lower down were extensive patches of wheat, barley, and potatoes. Then there are fields of maize, fruit trees, and prickly pears, while at the base and on the banks of the river are orange and citron groves and fields of sugarcane.

On a hill to the north of the town is an ancient fort, now almost hidden by the number of creepers and small shrubs which cover its walls. It is called Huaccac-pata (Hill of Mourning). It is, I think, the place where Alvarado was defeated by the followers of Almagro [in July 1537]. The scenery round Abancay is enchanting. The temperature was sixty-six de-grees Fahrenheit at 7:30 A.M., sixty-eight at 11:30 A.M., seventy at 3:30 P.M., sixty-seven at 8:15 P.M., and sixty-five at 9:30 P.M.

The preaching of Dr. Taforo aroused the usual enthusiasm. He was looked upon as the representative of St. Francis, I of St. Luis [Aloysius] Gonzaga, [the patron of youth].

We left Abancay on the morning of the 17th, accompanied for more than a league by the subprefect and thirty other mounted citizens dressed in their very best clothes. Then there was a great farewell *función* and drinking of healths.

Having crossed a range, on the summit of which is a plateau more than two leagues in width, we made a descent to the rich valley of Curahuasi (House of the Heir), covered with sugar haciendas, in one of which we were hospitably received. There is also a small village. After an excellent dinner, followed by a delicious liqueur distilled from citron, I went with Dr. Taforo to the church. It was, though formerly with some pretensions, now in a most deplorable state of dilapidation and entirely without a roof, except a sort of shed over the high altar. It was the feast of "Nuestra Señora de los Dolores," and the altar was lighted up with a hundred tapers round a figure of "La Purísima" [the Virgin Mary] with a heart pierced by six swords. The night was pitch dark but the church was crowded and presented a remarkable scene. The bright light, with clusters of earnest faces grouped round the altar, contrasted forcibly with the profound darkness of the body of the church, while above, the dark clouds drifted across a pale moon and the roofless gable of the west end stood out in bold relief against the threatening sky. By the altar was the tall figure of Dr. Taforo descanting in eloquent language on the various perfections of "Our Lady of Grief," which very few of the Quechua-speaking congregation understood, but they looked upon him as a sort of inspired apostle, and when the sermon ended there was a rush forward to kiss his hand. I got a smile even from my priestly friend when I pointed out to him the untidy arrangement of the properties in the vestry.

Next morning we continued our journey down the valley of Curahuasi and after a league reached the verge of the precipice, which descends perpendicularly to the banks of the Apurímac. The descent seemed almost impossible. The road wound backwards and forwards with such steep and frequent zigzags that I expected every moment to be hurled down. At last the precipice became quite perpendicular and a sort of tunnel was excavated in the solid rock, about twenty yards long, at the end of which was the entrance to the bridge. It is constructed of *sogas* in the same way as that over the river Pampas and fifty yards across. It is full 150 feet above the foaming river, which, though very deep, dashes noisily along between the mighty barriers which confine it on either side. The *sogas* rocked up and down at every step as I crossed. On the other side I climbed down to near the banks of the river, at a point where a ravine conveyed a little stream down to swell its waves. Here a majestic scene presented itself. On either side the lofty mountains rise quite perpendicularly, with the waves of the river actually washing their bases and their sides so smooth that a blade of grass could not find root on any part of them. The strata ran up in clear lines at an angle of seventy degrees from the water to the summit. Across this terrific abyss, three hundred feet above the river, the frail bridge of *sogas* is thrown, at this distance looking like a single thread.[1]

From the bridge we had to ascend a long *cuesta* by a steep, winding road, which brought us to the little post-house of Banca, kept by a widow. Dr. Taforo first said the office for the dead at her request to benefit her deceased husband, and then we did justice to an excellent luncheon.

Two leagues farther, over a good road, brought us to the village of Mollepata, where we were received in a most prince-like manner. Girls showered rose leaves over us, strings of dollars were suspended across the street, and twelve of the inhabitants came on horseback to meet us. I was still honoured by being looked upon as St. Luis Gonzaga. From Mollepata is a view on one side of the lofty peaks of the snowy cordillera and on the other of a high isolated hill called Tilca. In the evening Dr. Taforo preached in the church and met with the usual enthusiastic reception.

In the morning, continuing our journey, we descended a *cuesta* and, crossing a plain containing two sugar haciendas, we entered the long and narrow but picturesque valley of Limatambo, bounded on either side by lofty hills, up the sides of which in many places are *andenes* or stone terraces fourteen or fifteen deep on which maize and potatoes are still cultivated. By three P.M. we reached the pretty little town of Limatambo, nine miles from Mollepata. We were hospitably received by Dr. Esquibias, the kind and excellent *cura* of Limatambo, who has renovated the church at his own expense. In the centre of the plaza is a fine tree on a mound faced with masonry, and in front of the church is a row of tall poplars. The town, like so many other sierra towns, is surrounded by fruit gardens and fields of vegetables.

Next morning we had an early mass and started for Cuzco, a distance of nearly forty miles. Two miles beyond the town is the Inca palace of Limatambo, correctly Rimac-tampu (Tavern of the Oracle). It is situated in a delightful spot, commanding a beautiful view of the valley, but only two walls and the wall of a wide terrace on which the palace was built are still remaining. The two walls are the one twenty-five and the other fifty feet long, forming two sides, and twelve feet high, built of a white limestone. The stones, though of different shapes and sizes, are artistically fitted into each other without mortar. In the walls at certain intervals are recesses about a foot deep and eight feet high, with single stones for lintels. From being on the outer wall, it is thought that they were used for stations for sentries or some such purpose. The wall of the terrace is also built of the same artistic masonry and is about five feet high and twenty feet in width. The interior of the palace is now a fruit garden.

Continuing our journey, we ascended a long *cuesta*, which brought us to a fertile but elevated plain entirely covered with square patches of maize, wheat, and potatoes. Scattered here and there are haciendas with tracts of pasture. After riding for two leagues over this well-cultivated tract of country, we turned the end of a range of rocky hills and entered the vast pampa of Zurite. It is called by Prescott Xaquixaguana, correctly Sacsahuana. Here was the great battle which decided the supremacy of the Incas over the Chancas. Here, too, were the rout and capture of Gonzalo Pizarro and old Carbajal by Pedro de la Gasca [in April 1548]. To the north, built on the side of a hill, covered in its whole length by *andenes* many terraces deep, is the little town of Zurite. The pampa is swampy, impassable at this season, and of great width, covered with long grass. A causeway has been built across it, about seven feet above the plain, quite straight and three leagues long. We were hardly halfway over it when a mass of dark clouds came rolling over the hills to the southeast, the rest of the sky being beautifully blue. The graceful white egrets which abounded in the swamp left their search for worms and, screaming shrilly, whirled in wayward circles over the plain. The flocks of sheep scattered in several directions ran for protection to a common centre and collected in round masses with their heads huddled together. The cattle left off grazing and bowed their heads to receive the storm. At last the clouds burst out in loud and sonorous peals of thunder, the lightning flashed forth, and the rain fell in heavy drops, while all the time the sun was shining brightly in the west. After about ten minutes the storm passed on, leaving us in the enjoyment of a serene afternoon. At the end of the causeway was the little village of Iscuchaca, where we found all the men outside the church dressed in long black cloaks with palm branches in their hands. It was Palm Sunday (March 20). On the south, among the hills about two miles distant, the little town of Anta was in sight.

Passing on across three fertile plains separated by low ranges of hills, we reached the foot of a *cuesta* as the sun set. The sky was deeply blue without a single cloud, and the moon was shining brightly. As we reached the crest of a range of hills it threw its pale rays over the city of Cuzco, which lay spread out below, lighting up the sides of the white houses and throwing the stately stone towers of the churches into shade. It soon became dark. I entered the city of Cuzco at eight P.M. and was received under the hospitable roof of General Don Manuel de la Guarda and his wife. The prefect had received letters from Don M. Cotes and General Torrico and had been expecting me for some days. Soon I had a good supper before me, and after some conversation I was shown into a comfortable bedroom, sleeping without a break for twelve hours.

Chapter 12

Cuzco

CUZCO, THE city of the Incas, is the Rome of the New World and, historically and archeologically, by far the most interesting city in America, north or south. Though in a tropical latitude (thirteen degrees, thirty-one minutes south), it experiences a cold climate owing to its elevation (11,380 feet above the sea), and in winter snow often falls. The changes of weather are very remarkable at Cuzco in the changes of the moon. The rain falls sometimes in the night very heavily and in enormous drops. March is the end of the rainy season. Cuzco is situated at the head of a valley nine miles long and varying in width from three to four, running northwest and southeast, and bounded by hills of no great height above the plain. It is covered with fields of barley and alfalfa for cattle and horses and, besides several haciendas, contains the small towns of San Sebastián and San Gerónimo. The city is at the northwest end of the valley, a little more than a mile in length and rather less in width. On the north rises over the city the famous hill of Sacsahuaman, on which the ancient fortress was built. This height affords the finest view of the city. The spectator looks down into the plaza and along the valley with its two little towns to the distant mountains, crowned by the glorious snowy peak of Ausangate. The Sacsahuaman is divided from the ranges of hills on either side by deep ravines through which flow the little rivers of Huatanay and Rodadero, which, passing through the city, unite at its southern extremity. All the houses are whitewashed, except the lower storeys when they are of Inca construction. They have one upper storey, a Spanish addition, and are roofed with red tiles. There are three chief plazas east and west of each other, and besides the ancient monuments the city contains several very fine churches and cloisters. There is another view of Cuzco from the alameda at the south end looking upwards to the Sacsahuaman.

The ancient city was divided into Hanan Cuzco to the north and Hurin Cuzco to the south. The districts going from the foot of the fortress to the east and whose names are still retained were Colcampata (literally, Top of the Hill), where according to [Garcilaso de] la Vega was the palace of Inca Pachacutec, [the ninth Inca, ca. 1438–1471] and, after the conquest, of Paullu, son of Huayna Capac [the eleventh Inca, ca. 1493–1525]; Cantutpata (Hill of *Cantut*, a crimson flower); Puma-curcu (Beam of the Lion), the position of the Inca's menagerie; Toco-cachi (Window of Salt); Munay-senca (Loving Nose); Rimac-pampa (Plaza that Speaks), where the royal ordinances were propagated; Pumap-chupar (Tail of the Lion), called so from being the end of the city to the south where the rivers unite; Cayau-cachi, formerly outside the city; Chaquill-chaca (Dry Bridge); Quilli-pata; Huaca-puncu (Holy Gate); and Amaru-cancha (Place of Serpents), near the Jesuits' church. The great four roads to the four provinces of the empire left the city thus: that to the north or Chinchasuyu by the Huaca-puncu, east or Antisuyu by the Cantutpata, south or Collasuyu by the Rimac-pampa, west or Cuntisuyu by the Chaquill-chaca.

My host, General Don Manuel de la Guarda, was appointed prefect of Cuzco by the present president, Echenique, to succeed General Medina, who held the office during the rule of Castilla and was an excellent administrator. He formed a small museum and public library and planted the alameda. His successor is equally good. General de la Guarda is a native of Lima and, as a boy, commenced his career in the Spanish army. He was on the side of Santa Cruz and was wounded in the leg the day before the battle of Yungay [in 1839]. It is still stiff and gives him a slight limp in walking. As a brigadier general he took the side of Vivanco and was sent against Castilla [in 1844], who outmanoeuvred him. When Castilla became president, he banished General de la Guarda to Chile. It was then that I first saw him. He visited H.M.S. *Collingwood* at Valparaíso in 1845 when I was a naval cadet on board. On the accession of Echenique as president, General de la Guarda became prefect of Cuzco.

The prefect is a man of middle height with a good presence. He has a fair, florid complexion, straight, rather prominent nose, brown hair, and is clean shaved. He is very genial, well-informed, extremely good-natured, and well-bred. His wife, rather stout, was a Landazuri of Arequipa. They have two daughters and two sons. The eldest is a very pretty and lively girl of fifteen. She is practically dumb but not deaf. It was an accident caused by her mother who, on receiving the news of her husband's wound, dropped the baby into a tub of cold water under the impression that he was killed. The nerves of the tongue became relaxed and she has never articulated since. We were very good friends. I talked a good deal to her and she easily indicated pleasure at what I said, or the reverse. Her name was Matilda. The others were small, the girl named Carmen, the boys, Manuel and Domingo, very pretty children. Our party was completed by the two aides-de-camp, Captains Martínez and Yabar. Martínez lived in the house but Yabar was a native of Cuzco and lived at his home.

There were two *tertulias* or evening receptions every week which were extremely agreeable, and intimates often dropped in on other evenings. The dean of the cathedral was a pleasant and very well informed old cleric and we became great friends. One of the canons, who is also rector of the university, was Don Julián Ochoa, a big man of a stately presence but most agreeable and friendly. The military habitués were Colonels Carriño and Moya. There was also Don Marcos Villafuerte, the sub-prefect of the city, and his pretty daughters; the Nadals, a large family; and very blonde and blue-eyed girls named Jara y Mendoza. Among the legal profession the most interesting was a Dr. [Francisco] Miranda [y Vengoa], who had been a soldier before he took to the law. He was a colonel in the Spanish army and Spanish aide-de-camp to the duke of Wellington during the peninsular war, and he spoke tolerable English. Full of anecdote, he was very amusing, but instead of evening dress he used to wear a blouse with full sleeves which the Señora de la Guarda did not quite like. He brought four nice girls with him, his daughters. Sometimes we had dancing. A large party came on Easter Monday to see the great procession of "Nuestro Señor de los Temblores" (very efficacious against earthquakes) from our wide balcony. It is a gigantic figure of Christ tied to the pillar, reaching quite up to the railing of the balcony. The prefect was in the procession in full uniform, along with all the other civil and military functionaries. There was a grand luncheon afterwards. A company of comedians was at Cuzco and acted in the cloister of the Jesuits' church. Each of the chief families had an arch which they fitted up as a box, the prefect having two. We all went several times and I visited the boxes of my acquaintances a good deal.

The lower part of the prefecture is of ancient Inca masonry. Above, a wide balcony runs the length of the house on which the principal rooms open. It faces the Plaza del Cabildo, with the old mint and the church of La Merced opposite. There is a long dining room and three rather grandly furnished reception rooms, with many others behind. An open balcony led to my room at the back, which would have been Captain Yabar's if he had not lived at home. It had a very interesting view over the upper part of the town with the church of San Cristóbal and the Colcampata. Captain Martínez had a room farther on.

I had several invitations for the evening at other houses, some of which I accepted. My most interesting and frequent visits were to the house of an old Dr. Bennet, who had been thirty years in Cuzco. It was in the Calle de Frisecocha, leading to the fortress. The old doctor, who is very well off, had collected a great many curiosities, including numerous vases, some standing two feet high and beautifully proportioned, two curious stone figures from near Puno, a gold ornament for the head, and two smooth golden bracelets dug up near Zurite.

Mrs. Bennet was a daughter of Colonel Astete of Cuzco, descended from one of Pizarro's warriors, who wrote a narrative of one of his journeys.[1] She is called the Señora Astete de Bennet and like the Señora Chepita is steeped in the traditions and folklore of the Incas. Her father was a friend of the *cacique* [Indian leader] Pumacahua, the Rienzi of the Peruvian Rome, and she can remember him as an old and very short man with a long nose and bright eyes. He could hardly speak Spanish but wrote it perfectly. He was shown the immense but untold treasure of the Incas by one who is said to have been the last who knew the secret. Led up the bed of the river Huatanay for a long distance in the night, he suddenly found himself surrounded by vases, cups, plates, and figures of pure gold in incredible profusion. He only took what was urgently needed to equip his troops for an insurrection against the Spaniards. Returning to Cuzco, he went straight to the Astete house. The señora can remember his coming into the room, wet through. The Indian who led him to the cave died without handing down the secret. The señora believes and hopes that the treasure is hidden forever. This fully confirms the story told me at Lima by Don Modesto Basadre.

The Señora Astete de Bennet is a most kind and delightful old lady. She has a niece named Rosa who lives with her, a simple, good-natured brown girl. The señora knows all traditions and she is my authority for the sites of Inca palaces when in agreement with my other authority, Dr. Ochoa.

I was not entirely absorbed by my social duties. They only occupied my evenings. I had resolved to devote three weeks to an examination of the Inca buildings of Cuzco, and on March 21 I began with the Colcampata and the fortress. Ascending a very steep street, so abrupt as to be made in the form of a staircase, I reached the small square of San Cristóbal. On the west side was the little church in which a relic of the saint (a tooth) is carefully preserved. On the north side are the ruins of the Colcampata.

On a terrace with a stone revetment stands a wall built of stones of various sizes and shapes fitting exactly one into the other. It is seventy-four yards long and seven feet six inches in height. In this wall are eight recesses resembling exactly those at Limatambo. They are too shallow to be used by sentries for shelter. They are not likely to have been merely ornamental. They were never used as doors, for this wall is a revetment. One only is a doorway. I think that these recesses, as well as those resembling windows, contained *canopas* or household gods or other sacred or royal emblems. In the centre of the lower wall is a slab with a mermaid carved upon it, now much defaced by time, which must have been put there by the Spaniards. The fourth recess from the west is a doorway leading to a steep, narrow staircase. Above is a grass field on a level with the top of the recessed wall, which is, therefore, a revetment supporting what is now the grass field, once a garden leading to and fronting the palace itself.

The remains of the palace are of very small extent but of great arch-eological importance. They consist of a stone wall forty feet long and ten feet six inches high, containing a doorway and a window. The masonry is most exact, the stones cut in perfect parallelograms, all of equal heights but varying in length, with the corners so sharp and fine that they appear as if they had just been cut and fitting so exactly without cement of any kind one to the other that a needle could not be introduced between them. The doorway supports a stone lintel seven feet ten inches long, while another stone six feet long forms the doorstep. The window is five feet ten inches from the ground, two feet three inches broad, and two feet eight inches high. The foundations and parts of the wall continue on for sixty-five feet southeast, but almost entirely demolished, the stones having been carried away for modern buildings in the city. Beyond this ruin are three terraces, one above the other, built of a rougher kind of masonry and planted with *lambras* and fruit trees. They reached to the base of the Sacsahuaman hill. The sacristy of the little San Cristóbal church is also of Inca masonry.

The Colcampata palace is the work of the Inca Yupanqui Pachacutec, at the time when he was remodelling the whole city. This is in accordance with the probabilities, confirmed by tradition handed down by Pumaca-hua to the Señora Astete and by Dr. Julián Ochoa. It was certainly the home of the Inca Paullu (son of Huayna Capac), of his son and grandson in the early days of the Spaniards.[2]

I determined to approach the fortress by the precipitous ascent of the

Sacsahuaman behind the Colcampata, because by this route I should enter by the strictly Inca work of Pachacutec and his son, forming the capitol of the Peruvian Rome. It now consists of three terraces, one above the other, built of stones of a light-coloured limestone in the same style of masonry as that of the Colcampata terraces. The first wall is fourteen feet high and extends in a semicircular form round the hill for 150 yards. Between the first and second wall is a level space twenty feet broad. The second wall is rather longer than the first and twelve feet high. The third wall is only seventy-five yards round its whole extent. Above it there are many carefully hewn stones lying about, some of them supporting two tall wooden crosses. Here was the citadel. Garcilaso mentions three towers connected by subterranean passages. They are now demolished, for not only have the stones been carried away to build upper storeys on the Inca edifices in the city, but numerous excavations have been made in search of hidden treasure. I think I made out the outline of the foundations of the tower called Paucar-marca near the north end of the third terrace. The round tower of Moyoc-marca was in the centre and the Saclacc-marca at the south end. Sarmiento laments the destruction of these beautiful edifices, the work of Topa Inca [ca. 1471–1493], son of Pachacutec.

The view of Cuzco from this point is panoramic. The city lies spread out like a map, with its handsome churches rising above the other buildings and the market in the great plaza crowded with Indian women sitting before their little merchandise or passing to and fro like a busy hive of bees. Beyond is the long, fertile valley with its two small towns, and far in the distance, rising above the lower range of mountains, is the snowy peak of Ausangate standing out in bright relief against the blue sky.

The length of the plateau of Sacsahuaman from the citadel to the other extremity is 440 yards, its width in the broadest part 100 yards. Many deep excavations have been made on it in the fruitless search for treasure, and it is now sown with barley. On the south side the position needed no artificial defence, being bounded by a nearly perpendicular ravine descending from the tableland to where the little river Huatanay flows down to the city. On the other side of the ravine is the suburb of Santa Ana. In a westerly direction the position is naturally defended by a steep ravine through which flows the river Rodadero and only required a single stone breastwork, which still exists. But for a distance of 330 yards, where the plateau faces north, nature had left it quite defenceless. A smooth plain extends to the rocks of the Rodadero.

Here there is a cyclopean triple line of fortification. It dates from the monolithic age, centuries before the time of the first Inca, coeval with Tiahuanaco, some parts of Ollantaytambo, and a few other cyclopean remains.[3] The work fills the mind with astonishment at the grandeur of the conception and the perfection of the execution. It consists of three walls, the first averaging a height of eighteen, the second of sixteen, and the third of fourteen feet. The first terrace has a width of twenty-five, the second of twenty feet. The walls are built with salient and retiring angles, twenty-one in number, corresponding with each other in each wall so that no point can be attacked without being commanded by others. The angles are formed so correctly that two are exactly ninety degrees, the rest between ninety and eighty-five degrees. The position is entered by three openings, named respectively the Ttiu-puncu (Gate of Sand), Acahuana puncu, and Viracocha puncu. They are so narrow as only to admit of two persons to pass at a time. One is in the centre, one at each end. The most marvellous part of the fortification is the huge masses of stone of which it is constructed. The angles of the outer wall are usually formed of one enormous stone. That at one angle is fourteen feet high, twelve broad, by seven and one-half deep. Another is nearly as large, a third sixteen feet by six, and a fourth ten feet by six. Yet these enormous rocks are made to fit exactly one into the other, forming a piece of masonry unequalled in solidity and peculiarity of construction in any other part of the world. "The element of grandeur arising from gigantic masses of stones produces a feeling of sublimity which is indescribable. It equals that of Gothic edifices a thousand times their size. They strike the beholder with a degree of astonishment bordering on awe. To have moved such enormous masses seems the work of a race of mortals superior in thought and power to this degenerate age. It is impossible, in visiting them, to avoid the feeling that you are beholding the work of giants."[4] Viewed from a little distance the great fortress of Cuzco presents a most striking effect. The walls are of a deep slate colour, now overgrown with cacti, a small kind of iris, broom, and other flowering plants.

The little plain in front, about seventy yards across, is bounded on the other side by the Rodadero rocks, at the base of which are the ruins of a stone building. The rocks are rounded masses of dark limestone, and on the opposite side to the fortress the rains have, in the course of ages, formed them into grooves, now smooth and polished from the many generations of boys and girls who have been in the habit of tobogganing down them. It is still the principal amusement of the youth of Cuzco of both sexes. On the summit of the rocks are a succession of steps and two seats carved out of the solid mass. The pampa on the other side of the Rodadero is probably the quarry whence the rocks of the fortress were conveyed, how we know not.

From the Rodadero a road leads round the brow of the Sacsahuaman hill to the Colcampata and the Plazuela de San Cristóbal, and from that

"The rocks are rounded masses of dark limestone, and . . . the rains have . . . formed them into grooves, now smooth and polished from the many generations of boys and girls . . . tobogganing down them."

point very steep parallel streets lead down towards the Plaza Mayor or principal square of Cuzco. I was engaged in examining the Colcampata and the fortress and taking bearings and measurements from the 21st to the 24th of March inclusive.

I devoted the 25th to the Plaza Mayor and some churches. The great square is very large and presents a busy scene at the time of marketing; but I believe it was three times the size in the time of the Incas, rows of houses having been built so as to divide it from the Plaza del Cabildo, the north side of which is occupied by the prefecture, and from the Plaza de San Francisco to the west. On the east side of the Plaza Mayor is the cathedral, a handsome stone edifice, the see of a bishop with a dean and ten canons. It is certainly on the site of an Inca palace or hall or temple, said to have been that of Viracocha [the eighth Inca]. Opposite is the splendid church of the Jesuits, the finest in Peru, built in beautiful proportions, with two towers and a large dome over the centre; the façade is enriched by elaborately carved stonework. The cloisters are fine and have many pleasant reminiscences for me when used as a theatre.

The church of La Merced in the Plaza del Cabildo is interesting from being the burial place of both Almagros, father and son. It contains a cloister with an upper storey of exquisite beauty. The pillars are elaborately and richly carved, and the whole effect is most striking.

The religious orders of Dominicans (1534), Franciscans (1534), and Mercedarians (1537) still possess their full complement of monks at Cuzco, but the Augustinians have been suppressed and their church and convent are falling to ruin. In Cuzco there is a university, that of San Antonio Abad, founded in 1598 by the fifth [sic, fourth] bishop as a college and raised to the rank of a university in 1692 by Pope Innocent XII. There is also a Colegio de Ciencias y Artes, the college of San Francisco, and three schools of San Borja, San Andrés, and la Compañía. There are three nunneries: of Santa Catalina, on the site of the convent of Virgins of the Sun (Acllahuasi), of Santa Teresa, and of Santa Clara. Their inmates work really very excellent cotton lace, an art well known to the Incas, as well as open-worked mittens and gloves.

On the 26th I was in and round the Calle del Triunfo most of the day. Here are the ruins which are said to have been the palace of Inca Rocca. The first five Incas had their residences within the precincts of the Inticancha or Temple of the Sun. Inca Rocca, the sixth, was the first to conceive the idea of an imperial city, to establish *yachayhuasi* or schools, to bring a water supply by aqueducts, and to build a separate palace. There is reason to think that there was an edifice of the monolithic age, long before the Incas, which the Inca Rocca adapted. The wall is constructed of huge masses of stone of various shapes and sizes, one of them having twelve sides, but fitting to each other with astonishing exactness, though the exterior surfaces are rough and of a dark slate colour, like the stones of the fortress.

The college of San Borja and the church of the Nazarenes occupied me on the 27th. The former is a handsome building near the cathedral for the education of Indian children of noble birth. Túpac Amaru (Condorcanqui) was educated here. When the Jesuits were expelled in 1767 the institution fell into decay. A grand ball was given in it by Bolívar after the battle of Ayacucho. A portion is now used for a boys' school, the rest falling to ruins. The church of the Nazarenes is built on the beautiful masonry of the walls of an Inca edifice which have a peculiar interest, for seven of them have serpents carved on their surfaces in relief. There is a narrow street leading south from the Jesuits' church, which is of Inca masonry for its whole length on both sides, about eighteen feet high, with Spanish upper storeys. On a huge stone lintel over a door now walled up, two much larger serpents are carved. In the same street as the church of the Nazarenes, the Inca wall is supposed to be part of the palace of the Inca Topa Yupanqui.

On the 28th of March I continued my examination of Inca buildings.

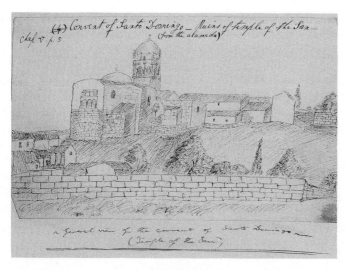

"The beautiful masonry is twenty feet high and in a slightly curved form."

The edifice at the corner of the plaza is supposed to be the palace of the Inca Huascar [the twelfth Inca, ca. 1525–1532]. The house of Garcilaso de la Vega is in the Calle del Triunfo, according to Dr. Ochoa and the Señora Astete, but this is wrong. Garcilaso's house was in the prefecture plaza west side. The [Calle del Triunfo] house was once evidently very handsome but is now given up to the poorest people. The walls of the inner court are built with Incarial stones, now clumsily put together. In this court, forming the door-post to an empty room, are four slabs. On the two upper ones two harpies are carved in bold relief; on the two lower ones are griffins with tails coiled up behind, certainly later Spanish work. Near this house are the walls of the convent of the Virgins of the Sun, over which has been built the nunnery of Santa Catalina, founded in 1599. The masonry is beautifully cut and in regular lines, as is all the Inca masonry in Cuzco, except the outer wall of the Colcampata and the palace of Inca Rocca. Following down the street of Santa Catalina is a wider street at right angles called Pampa Moroni, with Inca walls for its whole length.

The examination of the convent of Santo Domingo, on the site of the Temple of the Sun, occupied me for three days. The open space in front of the church was once the famous Intipampa (Place of the Sun) where there was the circle for observing the sun, called Intihuatana. It is very difficult to realize the position and surroundings of the once magnificent Coricancha (Place of Gold). The church occupies the position of the principal façade of the temple, forming the south side of the Intipampa. The other

three sides are all formed of Inca masonry and, I believe, were the temples
of inferior deities, the moon, rainbow, thunder, and lightning, so that we
may imagine the Intipampa to have had temples on all four sides, with a
circle and short pillar for observing the sun in the centre. The sides are
now occupied by little fruit and vegetable stalls and blacksmiths' shops.
The church is a plain edifice built of the temple stones, but badly and
clumsily put together. Its only redeeming point is a very handsome tower
with a number of elaborately carved pillars clustering round each corner
and between the arched windows. At the west end of the church is the
sacristy, which overlooks the river Huatanay and is part of the ancient
temple. The beautiful masonry is twenty feet high and in a slightly curved
form. Behind the church are a large cloister, refectory, and smaller
cloister beyond. The large cloister has an upper storey. In passages and
corners there are still bits of the temple masonry, but the whole place
swarms with Dominican monks:

> Bats make their nests in the temples of Manco
> And owls screech in the halls of Pachacutec.

Along the exterior wall of the cloisters, on the east side, is a narrow lane
running south from the Intipampa (Plazuela de Santo Domingo). Here we
have the whole of one side of the temple, quite entire, sixty yards long and
twenty feet high, over which the upper storey of the cloister has been
built. This is the finest piece of Inca masonry in Cuzco that remains. The
stones vary in length, generally two feet and one foot four inches in
height, most exactly and accurately cut, placed in straight lines, with their
exterior surfaces projecting very slightly and slanting off at the sides. The
architect had discovered sublimity and grandeur in the perfect symmetri-
cal combination of the simplest materials.

There is an extensive piece of ground south of the temple, between the
rivers Huatanay and Rodadero and extending to their junction. Here
there may have been residential edifices for priests and Incas. But it was
mainly occupied by the gardens of the sun, with terraces full of flowers
descending to the banks of the Huatanay. In one sacred spot were the
golden fruits and flowers, some of which I was privileged to see in the
house of Don M. Cotes at Lima. I was occupied in the convent of Santo
Domingo from the 29th to the 31st of March inclusive, examining, measuring, and making a plan.

Cuzco is closely connected with its river Huatanay, which rises far beyond the Sacsahuaman in a lonely ravine. It flows noisily past the moss-
grown walls of the nunnery of Santa Teresa, under the houses on the west
side of the Plaza Mayor, down the centre of a broad street, where it is
crossed by several stone bridges, round the base of the hill on which the

temple of the sun stood, and eventually unites with the Rodadero to the south of the gardens of the sun.

On the 2d of April I went up to the suburb of Carmenca to search for the place where the other sun observatory stood, which is described by several old writers. I met with no success but I was well rewarded for my walk, for entering the little church of Santa Ana I found that its walls were lined by large pictures of the utmost interest. They represent the procession of Corpus Christi at Cuzco in 1570. They give authentic representations of the gala dresses of the Incas at that time. First march the religious orders of Dominicans, Franciscans, Augustinians, and Mercedarians, followed by the Santísimo under a canopy, with an old cavalier in black, the insignia of Alcántara on his shoulder: I think the viceroy, [Francisco de] Toledo. Then follow the representatives of all the Cuzco parishes, each dragging their patron saint on a cart. They are preceded by the principal Inca noble of each parish in full national costume. On his head is a sort of turban surmounted by feathers and adorned with the imperial fringe. Round the neck is a broad collar of various colours with a yellow fringe. The tunic is of fine white cotton covered with ornaments, and round the waist is a broad belt of richly worked cloth. Garters of the same material confine the black breeches above the knees. Shoes were of black cloth. On the breast was a golden sun, illustrating the use of the golden sun shown me by the president at the house of Don M. Cotes at Lima. Pumas' heads of gold ornamented with emeralds secured a long crimson cloak on the shoulders. The tunic has full white sleeves bordered with lace. In one picture there is a *ñusta* or princess in nearly the same dress, with a page in front carrying her headdress. The concluding picture represents the return of the Santísimo to the cathedral, with the whole Inca family looking on, magnificently dressed. The heads and shoulders of the crowd are grouped along the lower parts of the pictures: Spaniards in black cloaks and broad-brimmed hats mingled with Indian men and women in characteristic costumes. The houses along the line of march have rich carpets hanging from the upper windows to the ground and the balconies are adorned with pictures of saints. At intervals there are a triumphal arch and a temporary altar covered with silver. The artist must have been a student both of the Spanish and Flemish masterpieces for his work has much merit. The interest attaching to the pictures is very great, for they are quite unique in what they represent. The *cura* of Santa Ana was very civil in explaining the pictures and much pleased at the interest I took in them.[5]

From the 4th to the 8th of April I was busily engaged on a plan of the city, with special reference to positions of ancient buildings. In that time I went twice to dear old Doña Astete's house to pass the evening. She had been very kind in collecting things for me, including sayings of Dr.

Lunarejo, the great Quechua scholar, an old Spanish map of the province, and Quechua songs. She had also had me measured for the dress of a Cuzco Indian, and now two dresses were ready, suits for a man and for a woman. I was extremely interested in the people, which she encouraged and told me all the good she knew of them. I put on the man's dress and went to one of the prefect's evening receptions in it, at which the Señora de la Guarda was no more pleased than at old Miranda's blouse, but the others were much amused, especially Matilda and Carmen.

The dress consists of a coat of bright blue or emerald green baize, with copper buttons and short skirts, but without a collar; red waistcoat; and black breeches coming a little below the knee; legs bare and llama-hide sandals. On the head is a velvet cap fitting close round, with a very broad brim of straw covered with velvet embroidered with gold lace and various coloured ribbons. Slung over the shoulder is a little bag woven in a coloured pattern containing coca. The women are dressed in a white bodice trimmed with red braid; a blue petticoat; and round the shoulders the *llicla* as at Ayacucho, secured in front by a large spoon-shaped *topu* of silver; the same head gear as the men, except in going to church when they use a hood or mantle. The men are frequently handsome, with olive skin, straight hair in a pigtail, bright black eyes, a slightly aquiline nose, an oval face, and melancholy expression when grown up. Boys are cheery enough. The men are very slightly built, of good proportions, but often with a stoop from carrying heavy things on their backs. Some have ugly and forbidding countenances. The women are often very pretty, but old age comes upon them quickly. Girls have a rosy tint on their olive cheeks.

On April 9 I went to the university to see how Dr. Taforo was getting on. He was the guest of the rector, Dr. Julián Ochoa, who gave me a sort of fruit confection with liqueurs. Dr. Taforo had been so fully occupied with his religious engagements that he had only once been to a reception at the prefect's house. He preached for three hours on Good Friday, the congregation moaning and in tears.

I then went to see a young artist from Quito named Manuel Ugalde whose acquaintance I had made. He has got the patent from both the Peruvian and Bolivian governments for making waterproof ponchos and India-rubber bags for loading mules with *aguardiente*. He had made an expedition into the *montaña* of Paucartambo to establish an India-rubber factory and even reached the Madre de Dios in a canoe, but got capsized. He filled me with a desire to see the forests of the *montaña* of Paucartambo.

I was to set out on a tour in the lovely vale of Vilcamayo [also known as the Vilcanota] on April 12. The prefect and his family were also going there, but dates were not fixed and we had to leave our meeting to chance. On the 10th I began a long letter to my dear father, little dreaming that he had died on March 31. News of the calamity did not reach me until July. On the 11th I gave more of my company than usual to the Guardas and was very busy in seeing that all the gear was in good order and making preparations for the journey. It was not a final farewell to anyone, but I should be away a month.

Chapter 13

The Valley of the Vilcamayo

THE RIVER Vilcamayo rises at the foot of the snowy peak of Ausangate and is a main source of the Amazons. It flows north down a valley that increases in beauty as it descends until it becomes an earthly paradise where the warmth is not heat and the coolness is not cold. The river, passing about eight miles east of Cuzco, receives the city's Huatanay River. Eventually it reaches the *montaña* or tropical forests, unites with the Apurímac, and the united floods join the Amazons as the Ucayali.

On April 12 I left Cuzco on the Bdellium rather late in the afternoon, the Cotham in charge of a young Indian named Andrés, recommended by the Señora Astete, a *chasqui* (courier), she said, and the son of a *chasqui*. He was fleet-footed and easily kept up with the mules. We travelled on the Ayacucho road until we were halfway to Iscuchaca and then turned sharp to the right. Ascending a *cuesta* and passing over a broad grassy plain, we arrived at the village of Maras situated in an elevated region, with fields of potatoes round it. The old *cura* received me very hospitably and gave me a good supper and bed. The party consisted of himself, a young Franciscan friar who was his assistant or curate, and a very nice girl with a short straight nose and mestizo complexion, of course a niece.

The old man gave me an interesting account of Maras. The place had known better days and was formerly inhabited by several noble Indian families. It was the *encomienda* of Don Pedro Ortiz de Orúe, a Basque cavalier and a companion of Pizarro who married Doña María Tupac Usca, an Inca princess, daughter of Manco, the thirteenth Inca.[1] She was married from the palace of her brother, Sayri Tupac, at Yucay and lived at Maras. There are still descendants from her.

The view from the stone cross in front of the little church of Maras is very striking. A plain stretches away to the northeast, and to the north are the grand mountains of Vilcabamba, so full of historical interest, between the Apurímac and the Vilcamayo. The plain abruptly ends at the edge of a precipitous descent, and beyond rise the mighty Andes, sending their snowy peaks above the clouds. The intervening valley of Vilcamayo is hidden from sight, but the lights and shades on the mountain sides, cut by deep ravines, were very beautiful.

Leaving Maras we descended a very steep *cuesta* into the valley, which at this point is nearly east and west and about two miles wide, bounded on the north by the Andes and on the south by the cliffs we had come down from. There was cultivation up the sides of the opposite mountains several terraces deep. Every available spot is grown with maize, and down the centre of the valley flows the river Vilcamayo. Passing for two leagues down its left bank, I arrived at a bridge of twisted osiers thrown across the rapid stream and supported in its centre by a pillar formed of huge blocks of stone. On the other side is the little town of Ollantaytambo, built where the entrance of another ravine opens from the valley and runs up between the lofty masses of rock, advanced sentries of the Andes. Crossing the bridge and riding through the town, I was most kindly and hospitably received by Doña Josefa Artajona (or in full Ochoa y Manrique de Artajona), a cousin of my friend the rector of the university, and by her daughter Justa Rufina, in their maize hacienda of Componi.

Both the ladies were very sympathetic and cordial, telling me how best to examine the ruins. Justa Rufina was pretty, though with an olive complexion, only tinged with roses when blushing. Sitting on a stone wall with a water jug by her side, overlooking the flower garden, and seen through the stone pillars of the verandah, she was exceedingly picturesque. They gave me a good luncheon and we then walked in their flower garden before setting out with my Indian lad to explore the ruins. They are only just across the road.

The mountain of the principal ruins rises from the road in front of the hacienda to an immense height in the form of a sugarloaf, but with narrow plateaus breaking the steep slope to the south and giving room for the buildings. There is little left, and the unusual arrangements which were made a necessity by the peculiarity and narrowness of the sites make it difficult to comprehend the original plan. Moreover, the ruins are of different periods, some certainly belonging to the megalithic age.[2]

Ollantaytambo was the fortress defending the valley from incursions of wild tribes from the *montaña* to the north. It is the most interesting ruin in Peru whether from a historical or a legendary point of view. It was here that the gallant young Inca Manco repulsed the attack of Hernando Pizarro [in 1536], and here was the scene of the famous Inca drama of "Apu Ollantay."[3]

A ravine called Marcacocha, fairly wide, descends from the heights to the Vilcamayo Valley, and at its entrance two lofty mountains rise on either side, with the little town of Ollantaytambo between them. The limestone mountain to the north is faced near its base with small stones. A steep path leads up for three hundred feet to the first small plateau covered with ruins. On this little level space are five immense stone slabs upright against the mountain side. They stand endways and are united by small smooth pieces fitted between them. These slabs are twelve feet high and at their bases are other blocks of immense size, in one place forming the commencement of a wall. A block forty-eight feet from the slabs was fifteen feet four inches long by four feet eight inches by three feet. After a prolonged examination I came to the conclusion that this place was an interior, a great hall of the palatial fortress. A stone staircase leads down to another small plateau, which I also believe to have been an interior of this rock palace.

Immediately below this is a very remarkable terrace with a wall of polygonal stones fitting exactly into each other, the lower course of immense size. In the wall are eight recesses two feet two inches high, one foot four inches wide, and one foot one inch deep to contain the sacred *canopas*. At the other end the terrace is approached by a handsome doorway with a monolithic lintel. The sides are formed of three immense stones sloping inwards. A long staircase, hewn in the solid rock, leads down. In front of the terrace and portal, which I believe to have been the entrance and vestibule of the palace, is a succession of well-constructed *andenería* [terraces], sixteen deep, descending to the valley. They would have supplied the garrison with provisions.

Beyond the second plateau, which I believe to have been an interior, is an open space. This formed a court in front of the palace extending to the brink of a precipice which is partly revetted with masonry. Here there is a very beautiful view up the Vilcamayo Valley and the Marcacocha Ravine. Up the steep sides of the mountain are numerous ruined edifices built of small stones plastered over with yellow mud, having steep gables at either end but roofless. Some are perched on almost inaccessible positions, probably barracks for the garrison. The ascent to the summit was very difficult and required a good head, but here was the most interesting

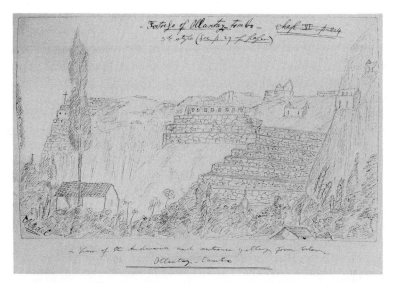

Fortress of Ollantay-Tambo — chap II p. 24
3rd style (see p. 29 of Report)

a view of the Andenería and entrance gallery from below
Ollantay-Tambo

" . . . the fortress defending the valley from incursions of wild tribes from the *montaña* to the north."

thing of all: an Intihuatana or circle and pillar for observing the equinox, like that which was formerly in the Intipampa at Cuzco.

In the little town, or rather just outside it, is the Mañay-racay (or Court of Petitions), 150 feet each way, surrounded by buildings of gravel and plaster, each with a doorway twelve feet high, surmounted by a mono-lithic lintel. The interior consists of large chambers, some of them open-ing into each other. The east side has been destroyed and replaced by a church, now roofless. These ruins are divided from the little town by a broad stream, tributary of the Vilcamayo, which flows down the ravine of Marcacocha and is crossed by the arch of a bridge.

The town consists of a few streets and a plaza lined with tall poplars. Many of the houses, with huge stone lintels to their doorways, are evi-dently partly built with stones taken from the fortress. On the west side of the ravine of Marcacocha is another mountain towering almost perpen-dicularly up to a dizzy peak. The two mountains form the giant portals to the regions of eternal snow. This second mountain is called Pinkuylluna (Place of the Flutes). Halfway up it are buildings most difficult to ap-proach which tradition says were used as a convent of Virgins of the Sun. They consist of three long chambers, separated from each other but close together and rising one over the other up the precipitous side of the mountain. The three are exactly the same, seventy feet long with a door at each end and six windows on each side. The doors have stone lintels. Two lofty gables once supported a sloping roof. There are windows in the gables and long windows in the sides of the buildings reaching up to the roofs. These structures are built of gravel and mud plastered over. If each window belonged to a cell, there would be eighteen in all. On one side of these buildings are three rows of *andenes,* each three yards broad, on which the doors opened. These may have supplied the inmates with food and flowers. About one hundred yards beyond the end of the *andenería,* the Pinkuylluna becomes quite perpendicular, a precipice about eight hundred feet high descending direct into the valley. It is said to have been a *huarcuna* or place of execution. There is a small building, something like a martello tower, at its brink.

About half a mile up the ravine, on the west side of it, the cliff becomes steep and juts out as a bare rock in some places. Here immense seats have been excavated and cut, with canopies, steps up to them, and galleries connecting them, out of the solid rock. One is called Ñusta-tiana (Princess's Throne) and the other Inca-misana from its resemblance to an altar.

After a very long day I and Andrés returned to the hacienda. Andrés had confidently relied on his coca leaves to sustain him. I was famished, but the ladies gave me an excellent late dinner and afterwards we had an interesting conversation until bedtime.

Next morning I started down the road to see the so-called tired stones and the quarry. What seemed to me most extraordinary was the distance from which the immense stones had been brought. The quarry is five miles off and on the other side of the river. From this point, which is high up the face of the mountain, these enormous masses of rock, after they had been accurately shaped, were conveyed down to the river, across it, and then along the other side to the fortress, finally to be raised to their present position.

The tools of the Incas, which have been discovered and analyzed, are usually of copper with a small percentage of tin, but it is evident that these would be quite inadequate for the work of shaping such stones. The first rough shape must have been given by some harder stone. Don Mariano Rivero, the Peruvian antiquary, has suggested that the smoothing and polishing were effected by rubbing with other stones and with sand, and that the finishing touch was given by means of an herb which contains silica, the *hippuris hyemalis.* These huge blocks had to be cut into various shapes to receive the dovetailing of their neighbours with the most absolute exactness, so that the measurements must have been made with extreme care and precision. When they were perfectly shaped they had to be conveyed down the mountain to the banks of the river, probably by means of cables made of the maguey fibres. The river then presents an almost insuperable difficulty. It is here nearly twenty yards wide and very deep, with a strong current. The stones may have been got across along a strong bridge of cables, parbuckled down to its centre, and then dragged

up by the united strength of hundreds of men. Then there was a distance
of two miles to the fortress and the raising of the stones to their present
positions. On the road there are still immense blocks which never reached
their destination, showing whence they came beyond a doubt. They are
well known as the tired stones (*piedras cansadas*; in Quechua, *saycusca
rumi-cuna*). The one nearest the fortress is at a distance of 460 yards. It is
nine feet eight inches long by seven feet eight inches broad and has a
groove three inches deep all round, apparently for fixing the cable. The
second is 170 yards farther off, twenty feet four inches long, fifteen feet
broad, and three feet six inches deep, like a huge beam.

I did not get back to the Hacienda de Componi until long after noon,
finding that my kind hostesses had got an excellent luncheon ready for
me. We talked long in the garden over some delicious lemonade and I
bade my friends farewell with regret. Ollantaytambo is a most fascinating
place.

I was going up the valley on the right bank to the town of Urubamba,
the chief town, only a few miles distant, so I could afford to start late. I set
out with Andrés and the mules, arriving in the evening. Urubamba is
quite a fine town with several good houses. Señor Valdez, to whom I had
letters, gave me a cordial reception. His house does not look much in
front, but behind it is built on three sides of a pretty flower garden with a
verandah all round. The family made me very comfortable. It was the
15th of April, 1853. Señor Valdez told me always to come to his house
whenever I was in Urubamba, staying or passing through, and he said it
with such heartiness that I felt bound to do as he wished.

On the 16th I rode up the beautiful valley to Yucay, where the Incas
had their country palace with baths, gardens, and all conceivable de-
lights. I was disappointed to find that nothing remained but a wall with
two of the usual recesses, though it is a lovely spot. In exploring the
neighbourhood I came upon *andenería* with walls of great age, certainly
of Inca times, arranged in patterns. In the rocky mountain above is the
great cemetery of Inca nobles, called the Tantanamarca. Each tomb is an
excavation fronted by a masonry wall with an entrance. They are perched
about in almost inaccessible places. I climbed up to one but found that it
had been desecrated, probably in search of treasure.

On returning to Urubamba, I heard of an Inca palace on the plateau
where Maras stands but at the other end. So I set out again, passing
through the pretty village of Huayllabamba. A steep *cuesta* brought us to
the plateau and there was a short ride to the village of Chinchero. The
cura, Dr. Rosas, was away, but the sacristan made me comfortable in his
house whence, from the back windows, there is a beautiful view over the
valley.

The actual site of the palace is occupied by a modern church, but the outer wall of Inca masonry remains with ten full-length recesses. The ruins are historically interesting because it was to the palace of Chinchero that the Inca Tupac Yupanqui retired in his old age, planted extensive gardens, and here he died.

I returned to Urubamba on the 18th. The governor is an Indian but well educated. He told me that the best version of the Quechua drama of "Ollantay" was in the possession of the old *cura* of Lares, a village on the other side of the mountains. I determined to set out at once to make a copy of it. The first thing was to buy a quantity of paper at a sort of general shop. Señor Valdez said that the best thing for me to do was to go that evening to his maize hacienda of Yanahuara on the road to Lares and sleep there. I took this advice and next morning I found that Yanahuara was at the entrance of a ravine leading up over the mountains.

Very early in the morning of the 19th we began our journey. The ravine, which was steep but picturesque, led up to a wild uninhabited *puna*. We passed two small alpine lakes exquisitely blue, and there was snow on the heights on either side of us. We then began the descent into a very beautiful country with a deep wooded valley on our left. The little tower of Lares church came in sight among the trees, and in the late afternoon we came to the *cura*'s house and rode into the little courtyard. There were two humble buildings at right angles.

I was received by a venerable old priest, and when I explained my errand he seemed pleased that I should have come from such a distance to see his manuscripts. He welcomed me and took me into the living room, which was furnished with a long table, a few chairs, and two old chests. It was hung round with portraits of Incas and some coats of arms. The reigning Incas were partly from Herrera's frontispiece, but the portraits of the later ones seemed to be original and interesting. The Incas had broad bands of black cloth round their knees, fringed above with red. They are not in breeches as in Santa Ana. They had a battle axe in one hand and a shield with a rainbow painted on it in the other, gold earrings, and two feathers on their turbans, which are black and white. They all had the red fringe on their foreheads. Each had a motto.

The *cura* of Lares was Dr. Don Pablo Policarpo Justiniani, a descendant of the Incas, his great-grandfather having married a daughter of the princess who was wife to Ortiz de Orúe of Maras. He showed me the pedigree and also the Justiniani pedigree, showing his descent from the Emperor Justinian through the Genoese family. He brought out the manuscript of the drama of "Apu Ollantay." It was the original document, belonging to that *cura* of Sicuani who was the friend of Túpac Amaru (Condorcanqui). He was the first to take the drama down from the mouths of learned Indians and to divide it into acts and scenes. Dr. Rosas of Chinchero has a copy and there is one in the library of the monastery of Santo Domingo at Cuzco. But this is the original. He also brought out a book of Quechua songs. He gave me leave to copy any of his manuscripts, so I got out the Urubamba paper and set to work at once. It occupied me for four evenings, from the 19th to the 23d of April.

There was one other inmate, a good-natured brown girl with bright eyes who brought in the meals and waited, assisted by Andrés, but also messed with us. For supper there was a fairly well cooked *chupé* and chocolate that I had brought with milk. Afterwards we conversed about Incas and Justinianis until the old man said he had a bad headache, when the girl came in and stuck coca leaves all over his temples and forehead, and he went to bed with a green forehead. Next morning the leaves had quite cured him, but he retired again with a green forehead on the 21st. I went on copying, with a tallow candle, until past midnight. My bed was conveniently placed by Andrés just behind the chair in which I was copying. It consisted of the *pellón* off the mule.

In the daytime I took long walks and enquired into the domestic economy of the people of Lares. Up a ravine of wondrous beauty is a medicinal spring with a building over it and some rooms or rather cabins. I also had a delightful walk down the valley of the Yanatile, a tributary of the Vilcamayo, flowing north-northeast.

My numerous conversations with Dr. Justiniani enabled me to acquire a large stock of Inca lore, and he enlightened me respecting many things. He was a dear old man and most interesting. On Wednesday forenoon I had finished the copying and was packing the saddlebags when the girl rushed in, declaring, to my astonishment, that General de la Guarda was there. I ran out and there, sure enough, was the prefect, his two aides-de-camp, an orderly, and a friend who had come to take the waters. They insisted on my coming back with them to Calca, a town in the valley above Yucay. So after a rest we started. They went a good pace, anxious to get back into the valley before dark. But Andrés easily kept up with them. He was a fleet-footed lad.

Then followed six days of prefectorial dissipation. There was a large dinner party at Calca, and next morning we started for Urubamba, where the prefect's family was staying, accompanied by the subprefect and thirty cavaliers on horseback. Crowds lined the roads and everywhere the national bicolour was flying. Riding down the street of Urubamba I saw the young Franciscan friar and the nice girl from Maras in a doorway and just had time to greet them as my mule was hurried past in the crowd of horsemen. But I do not like her being so much with that friar. In the evening of the 25th there was another grand dinner at Urubamba. Señor Valdez was rather embarrassing. I had told him and his family many anecdotes and indulged in witticisms and bons mots. At the dinner party his sentences usually began, "De todas las cuentas de Don Clemente lo mejor es" [Of all Don Clemente's stories the best is], and then came a startling version of one of my stories. I never knew what was coming next.

On the 26th we all went to Ollantaytambo on my second visit. The prefect's party was in a house in the town and I went to my friends, the Artajonas. It was very pleasant, though a grown-up son was there who was rather a wet blanket. I again went over the ruins, with the Guarda children and Dr. Taforo, who was one of the prefect's guests at Urubamba and Ollantaytambo. Returning to Urubamba we were invited to an afternoon party at the maize hacienda of Señora Ampuero. She was a good entertainer and the whole arrangement was excellent. There was no sit-down meal but plenty of refreshments and dancing. It was a very good country house, and in front of the verandah was a tower for disengraining the maize.

Here I met Dr. [José] La Puerta, a judge of the supreme court at Lima, a shrewd, clever lawyer, and his half-brother, Don Manuel Novoa, sub-prefect of the province of Canas, with a good house at Cuzco. The latter is a tall, handsome man with long grey hair, genial and courteous. With him was his daughter aged twelve, a cheery girl with fair complexion and rosy cheeks, a straight, prominent nose, and brown hair in two long tails.[4] As I was destined to travel with these people across the Andes to Arequipa, I will here record their ancestry and connections.

The father of Don Manuel Novoa was a Spaniard named Don Santiago Novoa who settled at Cuzco. His ancestors were from Galicia and one of them was at the battle of Las Navas de Tolosa in 1313 [*sic*, 1212]. Don Santiago married the Countess Gertrudis Mendoza y Jara, sister of the bishop of Cuzco, 1838–54. She married secondly Don Santiago La Puerta. By the first marriage she had Don Manuel Novoa; by the second, Dr. Don José La Puerta, judge of the supreme court, and General Don Luis La Puerta, vice-president of the republic, 1876–79. Don Manuel Novoa married a widow, Doña María del Pilar de la Bellota, who had had three children by her first husband named Gálvez: Felipe, Antonio, and Melchora, married to Don Isaac Castro of Abancay, both dead. By Doña María del Pilar, Don Manuel Novoa had two daughters: Victoria, my friend, and Antonia. Victoria's mother was a daughter of Colonel Don Melchior de la Bellota who was slain at the battle of Vilquepuquio and a descendant of the dukes of Bejar.

Don Manuel Novoa, hearing that I was going into the *montaña,* called my attention to the great commercial and medicinal value of the *cascarilla* trees (*chinchona genus*) and advised me to look out for them.

I passed an exceedingly pleasant afternoon at the party given by Señora Ampuero and returned with the Guardas to Urubamba. Next day the prefect and his family returned to Cuzco and I set out for Pisac on my way to the *montaña* of Paucartambo.

It is a long though a most lovely ride up the valley to Pisac, and I was delayed by visiting the Ampuero hacienda again and lingering at Yucay. It was getting late when I arrived and there were some important ruins to examine. Perched on steep rocks is a fortress with many *andenería*. But the relic of chief interest is a very perfect Intihuatana. It is within walls having recesses like those on the terrace at Ollantaytambo. Pisac and Ollantaytambo were the two palatial fortresses to defend the valley of the Vilcamayo, the one against invasions from the Collao to the south, the other from invasions of wild tribes of Indians from the *montaña* to the north.

It was dark when I left the ruins and I knew of no lodging to go to in Pisac. But Andrés was a lad of resource. A bridge across the river Vilcamayo connects Pisac with Taray. He went across and came back to me with an invitation from the governor of Taray to pass the night at his house, which I did. Next day my destination was Paucartambo.

Chapter 14

Montaña of Paucartambo

WE STARTED very early from Taray. To traverse the road, a rough and mountainous one, occupied the whole day. As we approached the town of Paucartambo, on a river of the same name, I saw several cavaliers diverging from various directions to the stone bridge leading into the town. I found afterwards that the prefect had announced my coming and its object and these *hacendados* (owners of estates in the neighbourhood) had been invited to come and meet me. Thus I was cordially received by the subprefect and met all these local gentry, who were full of information about the *montaña*. They were entertained at a supper, and on their departure I was shown into a fairly comfortable bedroom.

The easternmost range of the Andes sinks down to the vast tropical forest of the Amazonian basin. To the south, in Bolivia and Carabaya, the descent is gradual, the spurs of the Andes extending out for forty or fifty miles. But the Andes of Paucartambo descend very abruptly from a great height into the plain. The river of Paucartambo has nothing to do with the *montaña* of the same name. It flows north through an elevated valley, gradually descending until it finally falls into the Vilcamayo, far down in its course. The ridge of mountains rising from the right bank of the

Paucartambo is the most eastern chain of the Andes and descends abruptly on the other side to the tropical forests.

My informants at Paucartambo told me that only thirty years ago there were many haciendas in this *montaña* but all, save two, have been abandoned owing to incursions of wild Indians or want of funds. They said that there were two routes, one to the hacienda of Cosñipata, the other farther north to the hacienda of San Miguel. I resolved to go to the latter, owing to the presence there of the friar, Bovo de Revello, of whom I had heard much. They said that the journey was very dangerous owing to the wild Indians and that I ought to have an armed escort. The hire of a mule is three dollars. I resolved to take one mule and one guide, leaving Andrés with my own mules at Paucartambo. They said I was mad.

On May 2 I set out with my guide named Quispi, our way leading down the valley for fifteen miles to a little farm called Acobamba, where I passed the night. On the 3d we began the ascent of the eastern range and accomplished it in a few hours: the summit is here only 13,000 feet. Then commenced the long descent into the forest by a difficult zigzag path. The route I had chosen is the most interesting because it is the one by which the Incas penetrated into the *montaña* as described by Garcilaso de la Vega and Sarmiento. The former mentions a district called Abisca, near the foot of the mountains, and the hills of Canacuy.

Gradually the slopes covered with long grass were exchanged for a subtropical vegetation. There were many beautiful flowering plants. I here saw a *cascarilla* tree and soon afterwards another. The species was *chinchona ovata,* not a valuable kind, but it made me acquainted with the genus. There were other very beautiful chinchonaceous and melastomataceae trees and shrubs with numbers of ferns. As it got dark we reached the tall forest trees and were in a tropical climate. It was quite dark when we came to the little river Chirimayu, where there was a ruinous hut. Quispi said it was the *tampu* or tavern.

Next morning we followed the course of the Chirimayu to a small clearing with a hut called Guadalupe through a forest of tall trees and numerous palms. The following day brought us to a large clearing with a hut of more spacious dimensions where all the labourers slept. It was called La Cueva. I slept soundly but in the morning one foot was quite wet. It was blood, and the people told me that a vampire must have come down from the rafters and sucked just under the nail. While they do so, I was told, they keep gently flapping their wings backwards and forwards.

Leaving La Cueva we crossed the river Pitama by a light wooden bridge and proceeded along the right bank of the Tono, crossing six of its tributaries. We were now in the level forest, with the great mass of the Andes rising into the clouds behind. We saw parrots, troupials, and curassows, and in crossing one tributary we saw downstream an unwieldy tapir (*gran bestia* or *danta*) browsing. It was a very long day and steaming hot. At last we came to a hill, isolated and with grass on the top, called Balconpata, whence there was an extensive view over the boundless forest extending to the horizon all round, except where the Andes rose into the clouds.

Quispi was incessantly stopping me to listen, with ear to the ground, which at last became exasperating. A few more miles brought us at last to the Hacienda de San Miguel, where I was very warmly welcomed by the good father, Friar Bovo de Revello, and Pedro Gil, the *administrador*. I had brought them some supplies, toasted bread, chocolate, candles, and tobacco. After supper I had a long and very interesting conversation with them, receiving much information.

Bovo de Revello is a tall, big man, in the gown and hood of a friar of the Carmelite order, with a rope round his waist. His face was not that of an ascetic: his bright, eager eyes suggested an enthusiast. He was a Piedmontese and had been a year in the Lebanon, three years in Jerusalem, then chaplain at a hacienda near the lake of Acules in Chile, and now six years in the *montaña*. He receives a tithe from the hacienda of San Miguel and $300 a year from the government as a missionary. He said that he had not yet been able to get at the Chunchos or wild Indians, that they are very hostile and constantly encroaching. He has occasionally seen and had interviews with them but had not got at them for purposes of conversion.

It is eight years ago since at eight A.M. the Chunchos surprised the hacienda of Huaynapata and murdered every soul. Two years ago that of Santa Cruz met the same fate. Attacks on San Miguel and Chaupimayo have been repulsed. In the San Miguel battle Pedro Gil had a narrow escape and a Chuncho was killed with his second barrel from the centre citron tree in the plaza. The Chunchos then followed some muleteers in charge of a child and murdered them near the bridge over the Pitama. In 1851 Father Revello had led an expedition with seven others. They crossed the river Piñipiñi and came to an extensive plantain grove. They had to return from want of food but sighted the great river of Amarumayo (Serpent River) or Madre de Dios. They lived for some days on plantains. In the same year Lieutenant Gibbon, U.S.N., came to San Miguel but did not get so far. In 1852 my friend Ugalde, with Pedro Gil and twenty others, embarked on the Piñipiñi in two *balsas* [balsa-wood rafts], but they were wrecked at the junction of the river Cosñipata. All were saved and returned. Revello soon afterwards made a clearing three miles beyond San Miguel, intending to establish a small farm with the assistance of a young priest named Quirós. He called it La Constancia. Going there one day he found the body of Quirós stuck through with arrows. As the good father said, you find an arrow through your body without having seen or heard anything.

The two remaining haciendas of San Miguel and Cosñipata produce about 8,000 arrobas of coca a year. Cosñipata also raises 120 quintals of rice. The pay of the men is 2 reales a day and 3 when working with the hoe. Coca is $4 to $5 the arroba, rice $3.

Father Bovo de Revello told me a good deal about the Chunchos. They are divided into three tribes: Tuyuneris, Huachipayris, and Sirineyris. The Tuyuneris are fine, athletic, brave men, chiefly on the other side of the Piñipiñi hills to the north. Their houses and a whole league of banana plantation, apparently abandoned, were found by Revello. The Huachi-payris are on the other side of the river Cosñipata. They are smaller, ug-lier, and more cowardly, holding the Tuyuneris in great dread, though in-veterate enemies. General Miller visited them in 1833. The Sirineyris are farther south, on both sides of the Cosñipata and in Marcapata. The ar-rows of the tribes are all ten feet long, with bright-coloured feathers fas-tened spirally. Some have points of *chonta* palm, others of bamboo and broader. They catch fish and cook them in green *ipa* or bamboo joints. They have a communal house holding fifty or sixty people. They make thick clay pots, and besides fish their food is almonds, yuccas, maize, and bananas.

Bovo de Revello undertook to take me to his farm of La Constancia, where Quirós was murdered, and if possible to a sight of the Madre de Dios. Quispi would not come. We had an early mass in the little hut used as a chapel and then started. There was a little path through the dense forest to the clearing of La Constancia, which was desolate: a scorching noonday sun, absolute silence, and thoughts of poor Quirós. It was rather uncanny. Beyond, it was a case of cutting our way through the jungle with machetes. In the end we did get a sight of the broad Madre de Dios after it had been formed by the junction of the Piñipiñi from the north-west, the Tono from the west, and the Cosñipata from the south. It was a grand sight. The Madre de Dios is the chief tributary of the Beni. Bovo de Revello thought it went to the Purus, but that was a mistake.

In the last evening at San Miguel the good father descanted on the great future of the *montaña*. He had recently printed a pamphlet entitled *El brillante porvenir del Cuzco*, the splendid future for Cuzco, when the wealth of the *montaña* becomes known. He spoke of cinchona trees yielding quinine which grow on the slopes of the Andes; of the India-rub-ber trees, a source of boundless riches; of the balsam trees, the *chonta* palms, and bamboos and their many uses, the *palmito* and its edible pith, grass for hats, and the splendid timber. Then, in imagination, he called up before his mind's eye the thousands of square miles that might be cultivated with coca, maize, coffee, cocoa, bananas, sugarcane, and cotton and the happy Christian population such crops would sustain in comfort.

Early next morning we parted as men part who are never likely to meet again. As I rode away I shouted, "Viva el brillante porvenir del Cuzco," and he waved his hand again and again.

Quispi did not conceal his pleasure at being on the way home. We pushed on and reached the hut by the Chirimayu, Quispi's "tavern," soon after dark. Next day I accomplished the long ascent very leisurely, stopping to examine plants, more especially cinchona trees. It was late when we reached Acobamba, and next day I received congratulations on my safe return from the hospitable subprefect of Paucartambo and his family. Andrés was very glad to see me again and so, I think, were the mules. I stayed a day as they make interesting things at Paucartambo: beautiful carved calabashes, spoon-shaped *topus*, coca bags (*chuspas*) woven in patterns, and slings.

On May 13 I took leave of my kind Paucartambo friends and started for Cuzco. My object was to gain the Puno and Cuzco road. Andrés took me to a little mountain village called Huasac, where there was a conspicuous Inca tomb; but soon afterwards we lost our way. At length, toward evening, we were at the top of a *cuesta* looking into the valley of the Vilcamayo, but we had no idea whereabouts in the valley. The descent of the *cuesta* took us down into a pretty wooded ravine and there we met several people taking a walk in the cool of the evening. There were an elderly and a young priest, another young man, and three ladies. The elder priest at once came forward and invited me, a perfect stranger but tired by a long ride, to come and stay at his country house or *finca*. A short walk brought us all to it: a large house with a chapel, quite surrounded by gardens, and I was shown into a comfortable bedroom. My host introduced himself as Dr. Don José Manuel Tapia y Guaycochea, *cura* of the parish of Sandia in Carabaya and proprietor of this *finca* of Vista Florida. One lady was practically his wife, which was a little irregular, but she seemed a well-conducted middle-aged person. The other ladies were her sister and niece. The young priest was named Ríos.

The supper was excellent and there was a plentiful supply of alfalfa for my mules. I spent the next day going over a neighbouring maize hacienda, watching the various operations and getting the Quechua names of everything. In the evening there were harvest festivities among the Indians which degenerated into a regular orgy, the young priest, Ríos, being in the thick of it and indeed the ringleader. I was kept awake nearly all night. Next morning he begged me not to mention this temporary forgetfulness of his priestly character when I returned to Cuzco.

Fortunately Dr. Guaycochea was returning to Sandia, so he said he would show me the way to the Cuzco road. There we bade each other farewell, I with many thanks for his great and spontaneous hospitality. We were soon at Cuzco. As I rode across the Plaza Mayor with the Chuncho arrows at my back, given to me by Bovo de Revello, I was very warmly greeted by the dean from his balcony and by other friends. The Guardas were very glad to see me. They said that Dr. Taforo had made all the arrangements for my journey to Arequipa and the coast. Señora Guarda had also written to her brother Señor Landazuri to receive me in their *finca* just outside Arequipa. I spent the evening quietly with the Guardas. It was the 16th of May, 1853, and I had been thirty-four days absent from Cuzco.

Chapter 15

Across the Andes
from Cuzco to Arequipa

THE DAY after my return to Cuzco was a Sunday. As soon as high mass was over I went to the university building to find out what Dr. Taforo had been arranging about me. He told me that Dr. La Puerta was going to Lima to take up his appointment as judge of the supreme court and that he had invited us both to join his party. Besides Dr. La Puerta and ourselves, we were to be accompanied part of the way by Don Manuel Novoa, by his daughter Victoria, on her way to be educated by French nuns at Lima, and by three youths going to the College of San Carlos at Lima, partly at the expense of Don Manuel. It was a large and likely to be a lively party. I thanked Dr. Taforo for making such an excellent arrangement for me. We were to start on the 19th in the afternoon and meet at Huaro, twenty-four miles south of Cuzco.

After Dr. Taforo had made these explanations, I had a long and most interesting conversation with Dr. Julián Ochoa, the rector of the university, on the subject of Inca history and civilization. On taking leave he made me a most valuable present, the manuscript of the Quechua drama of "Usca Paucar," the date of which he placed about the middle of the seventeenth century. Two years afterwards my friend Dr. Ochoa became bishop of Cuzco.

I then went to the Señora Astete de Bennet with Andrés and reported what an excellent *chasqui* he had been. He wanted to go with me but she thought it better that he should remain with his people in Cuzco; besides, Dr. La Puerta's *arrieros* would look after my mules. So we parted with regret. I had a last long talk with the old lady and Rosa, but the Bennets were going to Lima, so I should see them again.

The last day now passed in leave-takings and in having a last look at the fortress, the Colcampata, and the pictures at Santa Ana. The day for parting came and I bade farewell to the prefect and his family and the obliging, courteous aides-de-camp with great regret. They had made me at home and very comfortable and nothing could exceed their kindness. In passing through the Plaza Mayor I stopped to bid farewell to the good old dean.

I stopped at the little town of San Sebastián because a number of Inca families was forced to live there after the conquest. From a rising ground near San Sebastián I took a long farewell of the fascinating old city with a heart too full of regrets for words. I also stopped to examine the masonry of the Inca stronghold near Oropesa.

Don Manuel Novoa had lent me a splendid mule with the *paso llano* (amble) to go to the coast, so that the Bdellium and Cotham had an easy time, one carrying the cargo on alternate days, the other free.

It was late before I reached Huaro and found there Dr. Taforo, Dr. Julián Ochoa, who had come thus far to see his guest off with his son, a very fine young fellow,[1] Don Manuel Novoa, and his three protégés going to the college of San Carlos at Lima. They were named Bernardo Puente de la Vega, a very good-looking lad with florid complexion from Sicuani; José Villegas, a fair boy with flaxen wool instead of hair; and a little medical student named Berrio or the *doctorcito*.

Next day, after a long ride up the Vilcamayo Valley through beautiful scenery, we came to the hacienda of Chasquihuasi, where we overtook the baggage mules and Victoria Novoa, in a green riding dress and Panama hat, on a chestnut pony. Here we were to pass the night. Chasquihuasi is a large llama and alpaca estate and factory for making coarse blue cloth. The two ladies to whom it belonged were most hospitable. After going over the workrooms and yards of the farm, we all sat down to an excellent dinner with our hostesses, a very merry party.

We were to start very early, the servants providing bread and large bowls of milk to break our fast. Then we mounted and the long cavalcade defiled out of the courtyard of Chasquihuasi. There were twenty-two mules. We continued to ride up the valley for five leagues and then turned abruptly to the right, commencing a steep ascent to the higher land by a gorge called Cebadapata. On reaching the summit we came to the large lake of Pomacanchi surrounded by wild-looking mountains. The lake was full of ducks and wading birds. After crossing another range of hills, we passed the lake of Acopía and the little village of Surimani. Yet another brought us to the great lake of Tungasuca.

This cold and elevated region is interesting from having been connected with the last struggle of the Inca race against their oppressors. Here, in the village of Tungasuca, on the other side of the lake, Don Gabriel Condorcanqui (called Túpac Amaru) raised the standard of revolt in 1780. Passing through another village called Pampamarca, we shortly afterwards entered the small town of Yanaoca, capital of the province of Canas, of which Don Manuel Novoa is subprefect. The governor and *cura* came out to meet us.

Yanaoca is 14,250 feet above the level of the sea and consists of one street, a plaza or marketplace, and two small churches. We were lodged in the governor's house, a range of low buildings round a courtyard. The governor's wife and daughter were busily preparing a repast for us, to which we were all ready to do ample justice as we had been in the saddle since seven A.M. We passed a very pleasant evening, all except Villegas, who was crying at leaving home. Victoria proved to be a very festive young lady.

We passed Sunday, May 22, at Yanaoca, waiting for Dr. La Puerta, who arrived in the evening, bringing with him three little Indians, two boys and a girl. They are much sought after at Lima as attendants to carry the carpets of the ladies and walk after them when they go to church.

The town of Yanaoca is built on a grassy plain surrounded by wild-looking mountains, and flocks of llamas and alpacas were scattered over the landscape. This lofty district seemed to be fairly populous, villages occurring at every eight or ten miles. Sunday was a great market day and the villagers from miles around were assembled in the plaza of Yanaoca. It was a busy and interesting scene. Girls were sitting on the ground in rows, wearing broad-brimmed *monteras* and mantles of various colours, talking and laughing merrily. They were selling potatoes, *chuñus* [frozen, dried potatoes], ocas (*oxalis tuberosa*), coca, medicinal herbs, maize, quinoa (*chenopusterium quinua* [*chenopodium quinoa*]), chickens and eggs, cloth and cotton. Men and women mingled in the crowd and a continuous noise rose from the busy scene. Suddenly, a little bell was heard in the church: instantly a dead silence, and every soul on his knees. It was the elevation of the host. Each one crossed himself and the business again proceeded.

Victoria Novoa insisted on my wearing my Indian dress while she put

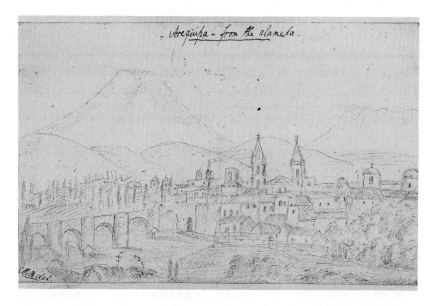

" . . . the white city . . . with the lofty peak of Misti towering above it."
(See p. 122.)

on my girl's dress. We walked about in the plaza to the great delight of the
people, and I bought a *chuspa* to complete the dress. After dinner Dr. Taforo, Victoria, Vega, and I played at a game of cards called *carga burro*.

On Monday morning, after a grand breakfast given by the *cura*, we
proceeded on our journey over the Andes. It was a lonely and desolate
road, always ascending, though here and there we passed flocks of alpacas and shepherds' huts. Dr. Taforo and Victoria enlivened the way by
singing, the one Chilean, the other Quechua songs. Under pressure I sang
"The Dawn on the Mountains was Misty and Grey." At last we came in
sight of the little village of Langui, where we were to pass the night. It is
situated on the banks of a lake several miles long, surrounded by mountains, their sunny summits reflected in the placid waters of the lake. It was
at Langui that Túpac Amaru and his family were captured and carried off
to Cuzco, to deaths of hideous torture. In the evening we walked along
the beach with the tiny waves breaking in ripples at our feet and the blue
expanse stretching miles away to the bases of the distant mountains. It
was a beautiful scene, the air so clear and fresh and the sky without a
cloud. Here and there the *huallatas* or wild geese with white plumage and
red legs were standing on the brink. They always stand in couples. Langui
is 13,640 feet above the sea.

Leaving the village early in the morning of May 24 and climbing a
steep zigzag *cuesta*, we reached a succession of still more elevated plains

and saw several vicuñas. We came to the post-house of Lauyarani very hungry. A girl supplied us with milk and boiled potatoes and brought out a tame little vicuña for us to see. She also gave me a sling for catching sheep and cattle. Then away the great cavalcade of mules went over the plains, with more songs from Dr. Taforo, one of Chilean gauchos addressed to death.

The country became wilder and more bleak as we increased the elevation. Here and there it was broken up into rocky ravines, with water frozen in their bottoms and patches of snow on their sides. As the sun was setting we descried our destination, a little hut called Huichuma. It did not contain any furniture whatever. Standing at the door of the hut, we made out two objects approaching. They turned out to be an old gentleman and his muleteer, both dressed in long ponchos of scarlet cloth. The former proved to be a Señor Fevres on his way to Arequipa. He was the manager of some of the estates of Dr. Goyeneche, the wealthy bishop of Arequipa. He was a pleasant-spoken old gentleman, always cheerful and rather an acquisition to our party. He and his muleteer attended to the cooking, made up beds, and loaded us with obligations.

The morning of the 23d [*sic,* 25th] was very cold, the air still and clear. The sky was cloudless and there was a hard frost. After hot cups of chocolate we left Huichuma and enjoyed the bright morning and the splendid mountain scenery. A ride of twenty-seven miles brought us to the little village of Ocoruro, the last on the east side of the Andes, at about noon. It is on a grassy slope and consists of forty stone huts thatched with *ichu.* The inhabitants spin their own wool and weave their cloth. The little chapel was in a most dilapidated state. There was nothing to say mass with and no priest had been there for many months. We were determined to have a mass for the sake of the people but the difficulty was to get the materials. After a long search, I found a few handfuls of wheat flour in a hut. By still more extraordinary good luck Victoria discovered two hand irons in a corner of the post-house. How they came there no mortal could conceive, but there they were. We heated them, poured a little flour and water on one, and then clapped the other on it forcibly. This produced some very fine wafers, which Victoria trimmed carefully with a pair of scissors and marked with crosses and glory round. Dr. Taforo then took them to the chapel and consecrated them. There was mass in the place for the poor neglected Indians for the first time for months.

Next we foraged about for materials for dinner. The Indians always say, "Manan kanchu" (Not got), whether they have or not, so we did not ask them but found chickens, fresh eggs, potatoes, and other materials for a *chupé.* Señor Fevres, assisted by Victoria, then proceeded to cook a most excellent one for dinner. Next morning, to our great regret, Don Manuel Novoa was to part company and return to Cuzco. It was a sad leave-taking for Victoria and a very sorrowful one for me, for we had become great friends. A very long journey was before us and we had to cross the highest part of the pass over the Andes.

A few hours' ride over a broad plain brought us to the foot of a range of hills which we ascended by a steep zigzag path. The poor mules were suffering when we reached the summit; we were not. It is 17,740 feet above the level of the sea, according to the measurement of Claude Gaye. From this point we had to press on until we reached the post-house of Rumihuasi on a wild height covered with patches of snow. It is 16,160 feet above the sea. After a short rest we rode on until sunset over desolate snowy plains, down into rocky hollows, up the steep sides of craggy hills. After the sun set it became piercingly cold, a keen wind blew in our faces, but it was a cloudless, starlit night. Until past ten P.M. we pressed on, half-frozen and peering anxiously into the darkness for the resting place. Several times we were cruelly disappointed by great boulders of rock. At last we came to two stone huts and a large corral surrounded by a stone wall which was the post-house of Ayavirini. Victoria was of the right stuff and game to the last, though the cold was intense. Directly we arrived she sprang from her mule, loosened its girth, and began at once to look about for the means of procuring supper. There was only one inhabitant who swore by all his saints that there was nothing. "Manan kanchu! Manan kanchu!" was his cry. At length Vega, one of the students, found a door-way in the other hut, blocked up with stones. We proceeded to pull them down and were rewarded by finding potatoes, firewood, and a quantity of llama skins. Villegas and Berrio had collapsed. We soon had a blazing fire and the potatoes in a fair way of becoming a very good Irish stew without meat. Under the superintendence of Señor Fevres and Victoria a fairly good supper was produced. Yet Dr. La Puerta was cross and even Dr. Taforo was barely philosophical, certainly not cheerful, for the baggage mules were far behind. As for beds, we did the best we could with the llama skins. We were all dead tired and slept well.

In the morning Dr. Taforo and I went to see a very curious formation. In the face of a cliff a number of tall columns rise up of a soft, crumbling white pumice full of small crystals. Some stood singly twenty feet high, others in clusters. They are called Los Frayles. Close by was a large pond frozen over.

As the sun rose it became warmer and we rode onwards over plains partially covered with snow. Several vicuñas were in sight. By noon we reached the post-house of Colca and had cups of chocolate. It was a long ride to the next post-house of Huallata, over leagues and leagues of wild mountainous country. We got there long after dark and were supplied with a sort of *chupé* in a large earthen bowl into which we all dived promiscuously with our respective spoons.

We left Huallata early on May 28, the whole day's journey being a gradual descent. The snow began to disappear, lofty cacti began to rise on each side of the path, and hardy wildflowers began to make the hitherto cheerless way look brighter. Toward evening we reached the posthouse of Apo and came in sight of Misti, the lofty volcanic peak overhanging Arequipa. The distance across the wild part from Yanaoca to Apo was 228 miles. We rested a short time at Apo and then pressed onwards down a steep *cuesta* into the vale of Arequipa and stopped for supper and to pass the night at the little farm of Cabracancha.

Early in the morning of May 29 we left Cabracancha and had breakfast at a farm called Cangallo, where we were waited upon by a young widow, who could not pass us by or bring in the chocolate or serve up the breakfast without repeating a verse of what must have been a very melancholy song:

La más bella niña / De nuestro lugar
Hoy viuda y sola / Y ayer de casa.
(The prettiest girl / In our village
Today a widow and alone / But yesterday married.)

Victoria said it was no use trying to cheer her up. Time alone could do that. So we mounted and, reaching the crest of a hill, came in sight of the white city of Arequipa in the midst of a fertile plain with the lofty peak of Misti towering above it.

Then we rode into the city. Dr. La Puerta and his party went to a house that had been hired for them. Dr. Taforo went to the house of a canon. I went to the beautiful villa above the city, surrounded by a large garden, where I was hospitably received by the Landazuri family. The last I saw of Señor Fevres was in a tail coat and top hat, holding a long candle in a procession of the Virgin.

The Landazuri villa had a summer house on the top of the stone vaulted roof commanding a splendid view of the city. The garden had long alleys of roses and jessamine and was well cared for. My room was on the ground floor, opening on the garden.

I went periodically to see how the La Puerta party was getting on. One day I found Victoria in the courtyard chaffing the three students unmercifully with the words, "¡Perdí mi juicio, señor" [I lost my reason, sir]! I gathered that they had been found out in some peccadillo, being out too late or drinking too much, and that the words were used by them as an excuse. I often went to see Dr. Taforo, but he usually had a perfect *levée* in his room.

One acquaintance I made was a Mr. Mardon, who lived with his sister in a house in the town. One day General [Juan Antonio] Pezet called when I was there and I had a long conversation with him. He was a very tall, handsome man, well-bred and agreeable. As a very young subaltern he was at the battle of Ayacucho. His father was a physician of French extraction who settled at Lima, took a leading part in the earlier phases of the revolution against Spain, but eventually went over to the royalist side and died in Callao Castle during the siege. The son had followed the career of arms and in 1853 was a general. He was exceedingly well-informed and took a very enlightened view of the prospects of his country. He said that after a military revolution such as the country went through to throw off the Spanish yoke, it was inevitable that power should for a long time be monopolized by military men and that they should misuse it. He was, however, confident that the civil element would gain the ascendancy in course of time. It was a very liberal and enlightened view for a military man to take and I was much struck by it. I spent a very pleasant evening in his society. General Pezet, some years afterwards, became president of Peru owing to the death of General San Román. Being vice-president, he succeeded in accordance with the constitution. I corresponded with him about my first Quechua dictionary and he helped me with the publication. Before his term of office had expired he was driven out by a bloodless revolution on the ground that he had been too subservient in treating with the commanders of the Spanish fleet on the subject of their claims. His expulsion was due to a Chilean intrigue. But all this was long after my pleasant talk with him at Arequipa. I passed a very agreeable time there, taking long rides to the neighbouring villages, thoroughly exploring the fertile *campiña* [countryside], and going to evening *tertulias* with the Landazuris.

I had noticed that Dr. La Puerta's chief *arriero* was a trustworthy man and considerate to his animals, so I presented him with the Bdellium and the Cotham, being very anxious that they should be treated well, having served me so well over deserts and mountains, in tropical heat and Arctic snows. I bade them farewell regretfully. Toward the end of the time at Arequipa I moved from the Landazuri *quinta* to the House of Gibbs near the bridge as more convenient for starting. The manager was then a Mr. [Charles Edward] Stubbs, with a young Peruvian wife, and there were three English clerks.

I was to continue the journey to Islay across the desert on June 18, and on the previous day I went to bid farewell to my friend and traveling companion Dr. Taforo, who was going to Chile. Our parting was affectionate and we promised to correspond. His was a most loveable character and Chile was fortunate in having so gifted a man at the head of its church. Some years after we parted he became archbishop of Santiago.

On June 18, 1853, I left Arequipa to cross the desert of ninety-five miles to the port of Islay as one of Dr. La Puerta's party consisting of the doctor, Victoria Novoa, the three students, a little cavalry officer, and myself. We stopped for the night at the little village of Uchumayo, twelve miles from Arequipa, on the banks of the river Chili, which flows through the city and fertilizes the plain. Next morning we passed over a stone bridge which spans the river and, crossing a range of barren hills, entered the desert. The sand is hard and forms a good road. But a traveller might easily lose his way, for the whole desert is closely dotted with hills of the finest white sand in the shape of a crescent. They are called *medanos*. We reached the post-house in the centre of the desert, called Cruz de Caña, before sunset and found it a palace compared with those in the Andes. There were several rooms opening on a verandah. We all sat down to a very decent supper.

Next morning we got up early and found it cold until the sun rose, when it was soon intensely hot. Don Manuel Novoa's mule was delightful and took me along as if I was in an armchair. By noon we reached the post-house of Cruz de Guerrero and had luncheon. From this point the road descends rapidly down a ravine, where the fine white dust covered us and made us look like millers. We were soon at Islay, which is surrounded by a desert. I was lodged with an English merchant named Gibson. Dr. La Puerta and Victoria were received in the house of Mr. [Thomas] Crompton, the British consul. In the evening I took a long walk with Victoria along the cliffs overhanging the sea, which she had never seen before. She was filled with admiration and astonishment.

On June 21 we all embarked on board the steamer *Bogotá* for Callao, arriving on the 23d. I was soon again established in my rooms at Morin's Hotel. Victoria went to Dr. La Puerta's house previous to entering the convent of Belém for her education. I went to see her there twice and we promised to correspond. I gave her a gold chain and locket with turquoises. She was a charming, lively, straightforward, and very plucky little girl, tall and well grown, but not old for her age. The three students went to cheap lodgings. Vega often came to see me, Villegas once or twice, Berrio never.[2]

I found that the Bennets had come to Lima with Rosa, so it was there I made my final farewell to Doña Josefa Astete de Bennet, who had been so exceedingly kind and useful to me at Cuzco. She gave me two good pieces of Inca pottery at parting.

I renewed all my Lima friendships again and began to go to dinner parties and frequent *tertulias*. The frigate bearing the flag of Rear Admiral Moresby, H.M.S. *Portland,* was at Callao. Henry Chads was captain, Fairfax Moresby commander, and dear old Jack Shears of *Collingwood* days was first lieutenant. The others were Marcus Lowther, a charming fellow, [George] Parkin, [Charles] Rowley, England, and [Robert] Parr. [John L.] Palmer was the surgeon, [John] Holman the chaplain, Fortescue Moresby the purser. I was made an honorary member of the ward-room mess and was constantly on board.

I explored the ruins of Cajamarquilla[3] in the Rimac Valley with Lowther and afterwards with the chaplain and a little midshipman named Heron Maxwell, a good rider. I also took F. Moresby to Lurín and went with Palmer and some other "Portlands" to Chorrillos, where they painted the town red. One thing they did was to run a race across the town over walls, roofs, and backyards, without going down streets. Palmer was handicapped by having a kitten in his arms. There was a great row and alarm but we got home without being identified. The new British minister had arrived, Mr. [Stephen H.] Sulivan, a nephew of Lord Palmerston who was very civil to me. Colonel [J. A.] Lloyd was also there, a great character who had been given his congé from Bolivia. Franco Seymour had given me a letter of introduction to him.

I had received no letters, but one day Mr. Brandon brought me an old copy of the *Times* with the announcement of my dear father's death in it. I at once prepared to hurry home and took leave of all my kind friends.

Leaving Callao on August 12, I was at Panama on the 22d, Colón on the 23d, and St. Thomas on September 1, where I changed into a larger steamer. [Frederick A.] Maxse was on board who had passed with me on board the *Excellent* [in December 1851] when we were rather friends. He was very sympathetic and a great comfort to me. He gave me his book of poetry, called *Alastor,* and we had long conversations. I landed at Southampton on the 17th of September, 1853.

Epilogue

HERE THE journal ends. Markham left Peru in something of a hurry, but he remained in touch with many of the people he had encountered, even though he returned to Peru only once more. He corresponded with them and met a few who traveled to Europe. In his manuscript he noted these encounters and in his footnotes provided translations, usually quite literal and consequently rather clumsy, of some of their letters. The contents related largely to family matters, providing the information for the genealogies that Markham zealously kept and corrected until the end of his life. They tend to focus on the deaths and other misfortunes of his friends and as a result make rather sad reading.

The most extensive of these genealogical footnotes describes the subsequent histories of the de la Guarda family, with whom he stayed in Cuzco, the Tello family of Ayacucho, and his traveling companions Francisco de Paula Taforo and Victoria Novoa. With regard to the de la Guardas, Markham wrote:

> In 1854 General Castilla began a revolution against the Echenique government on the ground of financial peculation. After manoeuvring for a long time in the sierra, he at last came down to the coast and

won the battle of La Palma near Lima [in January 1855]. General Echenique fled and for a time all who served in his government were persecuted. Several were banished. In August 1854 General de la Guarda was obliged to retire from Cuzco. He sought refuge in Chile with Generals Echenique, Vivanco, La Fuente, and the accomplished scholar and soldier General [Manuel de] Mendiburu. Don Felipe Barreda wrote to me on April 15, 1855, that as he never mixed in politics and always looked upon himself as a passenger who leaves to others the direction of the ship, he never suffered any danger in these revolutions.

My good friend, General de la Guarda, was not so fortunate. He wrote to me from Valparaíso on April 3, 1855: "The newspapers of Peru will have informed you, my dear friend, how my poor native land has suffered from a revolution, headed by two unprincipled men (Castilla and San Román). The blood of my countrymen has been made to flow in torrents, more especially that of the generals, of whom two are known to you, namely Generals [Trinidad] Morán and [Alejandro] Deustua. The latter was governor of Callao when you were in Peru. The other public men who remained loyal to the government were banished. I am one of those who suffered, but I entertain the hope, like all exiles, of soon returning to my native land."

From Santiago, he wrote on September 29, 1855: "I am very anxious to see the work on Peru which you intend to publish, as I have a very high opinion of your ability and industry. For the present I remain here, where I see almost every day our old friend Dr. Taforo. He is in good health and enjoys the esteem of his countrymen. I have sent your kind messages to my wife and family and I repeat that I am your ever faithful friend."

General de la Guarda died in 1873.

The Tello family also suffered from the 1854 civil war. Markham wrote:

> After two years and a half a letter came from Don Manuel Tello on October 22, 1855: "The joy I have felt in reading your letter has been made more complete by the participation of the whole family. I must now tell you of each of them and the mournful death of my dear sister Chepita, of the health of Manunga Ormasa, Mercedes, and Miquita, and of my nephews and niece; also of the anxieties we have suffered on account of a civil war which has unfortunately taken place in our republic. It is now concluded and the violent persecutions which I and many of my family suffered from the new government have ceased."

July 7, 1856: "Colonel Mosol is now in Lima and the young lady, Jesusita Canseco, rests in the bosom of the eternal, a victim to fever some months since. The young German, Vendelin, went to Pisco two years ago and has never been heard of since."

On October 31, 1882, Felipe Huguet sent me the news of the family, much of it very sad. Don Manuel Tello was a senator from 1860 to 1865. He married and left four children. He died in his house in September 1875. The Señora Mercedes died at Lima in December 1880. The Señora Manunga died in May 1872, aged fifty-six.

Of my younger friends the story was for the most part melancholy. Blas Huguet was a bachelor of Ayacucho University and deputy for Ayacucho, 1860–65. In 1866 he became judge of the superior court of the department. Felipe Neri Huguet entered the army. In 1871–72 he was military attaché in Prussia, Austria, and Italy. He was next colonel superintendent of police and in 1878–79 subprefect of Lima. He served in the disastrous battles of Chorrillos and Miraflores [in the war with Chile, 1879–1883]. In 1908 he was aide-de-camp to Don José Pardo, president of the republic. He died in 1912, being chief of the staff to President [Augusto] Leguía. José Antonio Huguet was a captain in the army and subprefect of the province of La Mar in 1865. He died of a very protracted and painful illness in September 1869. Agustín Zubiaga was attaché in Paris in 1865. He graduated from the university of Brussels. Doña Miquita's beloved child, aged twenty-seven, died in the fever epidemic at Chorrillos in May 1868, soon after his return to Peru. Estanislao Ormasa died in 1898 at Ayacucho, where he was engaged in business. Old Colonel Mosol died in 1856. The saddest event was the death of poor Agustín Zubiaga. He was the hope of the whole family and his death plunged them in the most profound grief, especially his mother, who was delivered up to the deepest desolation.

About Dr. Taforo, Markham provided more substantial details in a long footnote to his final chapter that mentioned a subsequent meeting between the two men.

Dr. Taforo remained a month longer in Arequipa after we left, but at the end of August 1853 he returned to Chile and lived at Santiago completely retired from politics and occupied solely in study. On December 1, 1853, he wrote: "How I have thought about you my dear friend and how happy shall I be if I find a place in your memory. But why should I doubt when I already have so many proofs of your kindness? This thought consoles me. I have always wished to visit England but now it is not for its palaces, its railroads, and its Thames Tunnel;

it is to see my young friend with his sweet character, his open heart, and irresistible good humour. In the letters I frequently receive from Ayacucho, Cuzco, and Arequipa I am tenderly questioned concerning Señor Markham. Farewell my beloved Clemente."

On May 31, 1855: "Your letter has brought me a precious gift, your portrait, which is most grateful to my heart. It has awakened in my soul the most joyful recollections. All our journeys came to my memory: the ruins of Ollantaytambo with its enormous masses of rock, the Inca-misana, the post-house at Rumihuasi, Los Frayles with their petrified wood and the frozen pond where we were so delighted by the icicles; above all Don Clemente himself on his splendid mule, with his great hat; all these things were brought to my recollection. Nor will you forget your journeys in Peru. Ah! they will never pass from my memory; nor can I ever cease to remember the dear friend who was my companion. He is the subject of my prayers for his health and happiness."

On March 30, 1857, he wrote: "I rejoice that you are about to be united to a wife you love and who is worthy of your love. The Señorita Minna Chichester is without doubt the wife that I should have desired for the worthy cavalier, Don Clemente Roberto Markham. I trust that you will present her with my respectful and cordial affection. From Chile I call down blessings from Heaven on yourself and your consort."

In 1858 Dr. Taforo was presented with a canonry in the metropolitan church of Santiago. He was installed on December 23d, 1858. In 1859 he introduced a young Chilean friend of his to me and sent me specimens of Chilean work, consisting of several cups and two bottles made of a bullock's horns.

At last Dr. Taforo came to Europe and we had the great pleasure of seeing him in Paris, where his bust was being taken in marble. He was also at Rome for some time. Returning to Chile he continued to increase in reputation and was acknowledged to be the finest preacher and the most liberal and enlightened churchman in that country. Finally he reached the high dignity of archbishop of Santiago, in which office he died. At least he was appointed by the Chilean government; but a refusal to confirm it came from Rome. This unjust treatment preyed upon the mind of Dr. Taforo and shortened his life. This excellent man died in 1898 [*sic*, 1889].

Markham also left a biography of his other traveling companion, Victoria Novoa, the young lady from Cuzco who had struck his fancy and who, in turn, seems to have been smitten by the young Englishman. The two maintained contact through letters for the rest of their lives. Like that of Markham's other Peruvian correspondents, Victoria's news became progressively more depressing over the years, for she, too, suffered a life that was marked by hardship and sorrows. Markham wrote in his final chapter:

> In 1855 Victoria Novoa completed her education at the convent of Belém at Lima and returned to Cuzco, her father having died the previous year. She married a young man named Camilo Chacón and had four children, Aurora, María Dolores, Mariano, and Agustín. Chacón was a gambler and took up contracts he was unable to fulfill, dying heavily in debt in November 1877. The creditors seized the deposits in the banks and everything in Victoria's house. This was done by the banker, Mariano Vargas, with the greatest brutality and inhumanity. He left her nothing. She was forced to sell the house at Cuzco, the only remaining property. Victoria and her mother, with the children, went to live in the Plazuela del Castillo at Cuzco in 1880. In December 1891 their flat was broken into by robbers and many things were stolen. Victoria relied on support from her surviving uncle, General Luis de la Puerta.
>
> For thirteen years, 1892 to 1905, Victoria did not write. In the interval her mother, General La Puerta, and her poor daughter Aurora died. Aurora left two sons.
>
> Then came the greatest calamity in poor Victoria's life. In 1905 Colonel Don Heráclio Fernández undertook an expedition beyond the hacienda of Cosñipata. He took with him his son Alcibiades and several others. Mariano and Agustín Novoa y Chacón joined the expedition. The colonel and his little boy lost their way and perished miserably of hunger. Mariano (aged thirty-two) and Agustín (aged twenty-eight) gallantly pushed farther into the interior with some companions and suffered terrible hardships. Their friends died. The two young men, with their mother's indomitable pluck, reached the foot of the mountains on their return. But they were like spectres, dying of fever, anaemia, and dysentery. They scarcely survived a month, kept alive with tonics. Their wives were entirely dependent on them. One left four boys, the other three girls.
>
> Victoria was left desolate with nine fatherless grandchildren and in the greatest distress. Dolores came from Lima to see her and tried to induce her to come back to Lima but she would not leave the children of her sons. She received £20 I sent her in March 1907.
>
> Victoria Novoa worked unceasingly for her children and grandchildren. At last she broke down; her heart failed. She was taken to

the hospital at Cuzco, where she died on December 3, 1915. Her daughter Dolores and two grandsons were with her. Her age was seventy-four.

In a series of letters written between 1908 and 1915 that are included with the manuscript and served as the basis for some of the above biography, Victoria informed Markham of her endless troubles, that her life was "always in an interminable chaos of hardships and afflictions." She wrote of the health problems that affected her eyes, nerves, heart, and sight; of another theft from her house in 1910; of her financial difficulties that forced her to give piano lessons to pay the rent and led to a request in 1914 for some sheet music, since in Cuzco she could obtain only tango music, "that I like very little"; and of the hardships besetting her family, whose maintenance remained a constant worry. Toward the end of her life she lost her religious faith, blaming God for her various and sundry difficulties.

Meanwhile, she continued to look on Markham as a friend, protector, and occasional source of financial assistance. "You are my best friend," she wrote in 1908, while in other letters he was her "beloved," "loyal," "unforgettable," and "much remembered" friend. In 1910 after thanking him for writing of her dead sons, she informed him, "I consider you a father of my poor and unfortunate numerous family." Her daughter, who had never met Markham, considered him "a father-protector and benefactor of the family." Victoria reported the very brief visit of two of Markham's young relatives, Alfred and Francis Markham, to Cuzco in 1908, their apparent dislike of the city, and their refusal of any hospitality. She regretted this greatly, possibly because it denied her the opportunity to show some of the gratitude she felt toward her old friend.

Victoria's last letter to Markham was written on November 28, 1915, dictated to her grandson. She began, "Dear tenderly remembered friend of my singular affection. I send this to you with my farewells and with tears in my eyes." She described the serious heart problem that had resulted in her hospitalization for six months, "and as I have no other help or protection than yours, no one to cast my eyes to," she was recommending to her children and grandchildren that they accept him in her place as head of the family until one of her grandchildren could assume that position. She concluded, "Adios, then, my dear friend; my heart remains with you and it is only an unhappy body that is leaving. Adios!"

She had not seen Markham since his departure from Lima sixty-two years earlier.

Notes

Introduction

1. Details of Markham's early life can be found in *The Life of Sir Clements R. Markham*, written by a relative, Admiral Sir Albert H. Markham. The book's chapters dealing with the trip to Peru were taken from either the original journal or this manuscript. Other details can be found in papers in the Clements R. Markham Special Collection, Royal Geographical Society, London, especially Clements R. Markham, "Journal, Sept. 7th, 1844, to Aug. 10, 1845," No. 2; Clements R. Markham, "Story of my service in the *Victory, Bellerophon, Sidon, Superb* and in the *Assistance* during the Arctic Expedition of 1850–51," No. 40; "Correspondence," No. 36; D. R. Markham, "Diaries of Rev. D. R. Markham 1848–1853," No. 24.

1. Pepperell to Lima

1. [Garcilaso de la Vega, el Inca, *The Royal Commentaries of Peru*, trans. Sir Paul Rycaut; José de Acosta, *Historia natural y moral de las Indias;* Antonio de Herrera y Tordesillas, *Historia general de los hechos de los castellanos en las islas i tierra firme del mar oceano;* Antonio de Ulloa and Jorge Juan y Santacilia, *Noticias secretas de América;* Joseph Skinner, *The Present State of Peru;* P. Diego Gonzales Holguín, *Gramática y arte nueva de la lengua general de todo el Perú, llamada lengua Quichua o lengua del Inca;* John Miller, *Memoirs of General Miller, in the Service of the Republic of Peru;* William Robertson, *The History of America;* William Hickling Prescott, *History of the Conquest of Peru. Mercurio Peruano* was a Lima literary journal that appeared between 1791 and 1795.]

2. [Johann Jacob von Tschudi, *Travels in Peru during the Years 1838–1842;* William Bennet Stevenson, *A Historical and Descriptive Narrative of Twenty Years' Residence in South America;* Robert Proctor, *Narrative of a Journey across the Cordillera of the Andes;* Archibald Smith, *Peru As It Is;* Peter Campbell Scarlett, *South America and the Pacific.*]

3. [Agustín de Zarate, *Historia del descubrimiento y conquista de las provincias del Perú;* Francisco López de Gómara, *La historia general de las Indias y Nuevo Mundo;* Pedro de Cieza de León, *La crónica del Perú;* Fernando Mon-

tesinos, *Memorias antiguas historiales y políticas del Perú;* Diego Fernández, *Primera y segunda parte de la historia del Perú;* Juan Polo de Ondegardo, *Informaciones acerca de la religión y gobierno de los Incas;* Pedro Pizarro, *Relación del descubrimiento y conquista de los reinos del Perú.* Markham was subsequently involved in the translation and publication of a number of these chronicles by the Hakluyt Society.]

4. My account of crossing the isthmus, interlarded with absurd stories told by Yankees on the way, was published in *All the Year Round* [sic, *Household Words,* February 12, 1853, pp. 521–24] by Charles Dickens. Mr. Watson of Rockingham Castle had made the acquaintance of Charles Dickens, who used to pay visits there. Mrs. Watson was a sister of my brother-in-law Captain R. R. Quin, who had been a lieutenant in the *Collingwood.* He showed my letter to Dickens, who was taken by it and said that he would publish it in *All the Year Round,* a little revised and with the characters talking more like Yankees.

2. Lima

1. [The *saya y manto* comprised a narrow pleated skirt, fitting closely to the body, with a hood that covered the head and face, leaving one eye showing.]

2. [Near Lake Titicaca is a place called Collahuaya, but, according to Baudin, the principal gold mines of the Incas were at Carabaya, Zamora, Parinacocha, and the Curimayo Valley. See Louis Baudin, *A Socialist Empire,* p. 108.]

3. [Pumacahua was, in fact, captured at Umachiri and hanged at Sicuani.]

4. [Markham's location of the house is inaccurate. The street, Jirón Ucayali, does not run into the Plaza de Armas.]

5. [Justo Sahuaraura, *Recuerdos de la monarquía peruana; o, bosquejo de la historia de los Incas;* Diego de Torres Rubio, *Arte de la lengua quichua.*]

6. The last time I saw Don M. M. Cotes was on the top of the pyramid on the field of Waterloo. He had been banished by Castilla as a friend of Echenique.

7. [The Peruvian currency was composed of pesos, also known as dollars, and reales. There were eight reales to a peso. At the time of Markham's visit five pesos were worth approximately one pound sterling.]

8. [I have been unable to discover exactly what the Colley Head Society was but suspect it to have been a society composed of young officers from H.M.S.*Superb,* on which Markham served in 1849–50. In Markham's papers in the Royal Geographical Society, the word "Bdellium" appears in conjunction with the names of shipmates who served with him on board the *Superb.*]

9. Charles Dickens made up an article out of my letters and called it "Leaves from Lima." It was published in *All the Year Round* [sic, *Household Words,* April 30, 1853, pp. 202–5].

4. Lima to Cañete

1. Ingavi was a battle between the Peruvians and Bolivians near Lake Titicaca in which the former were totally defeated and the president, General [Agustín] Gamarra, was killed. It was in 1839. Agua Santa was a battle [on October 17,

1842] between four generals, Vidal, La Fuente, Torrico, and [Domingo] Nieto, contending for power after the death of Gamarra. It was in the valley of Pisco. All four generals ran away.

5. Cañete

1. [Pedro Félix Vicuña, *Ocho meses de destierro o cartas sobre el Perú.*]
2. With reference to the estate of San Juan de Arona, the owner, Don Pedro Paz Soldán, had a son named Pedro Paz Soldán y Unanue who afterwards became a poet of eminence. His first work was *Cuadros y episodios peruanos* published at Lima in 1867, after a tour in Europe, extended to Greece and Constantinople. He wrote under the name of "Juan de Arona," the name of his father's hacienda at Cañete, vulgarly called Mataratones. His poems are redolent of the soil of the beautiful vale of Cañete as it was then and of the places on the road from Lima. In 1880 [*sic*, 1883] "Juan de Arona" published a philological essay, an exceedingly interesting work, entitled *Diccionario de peruanismos,* on words specially used in Peru, whether of Spanish or Indian origin, with remarks evincing much erudition.
3. [Markham is incorrect. No such law was passed, nor was there the deliberate policy of gradualism that he describes.]
4. [The arroba was both a wet and a dry measure. As the former it varied from place to place and according to the liquid, from 2.6 to 3.6 gallons. As the latter it equalled 25 pounds.]
5. [The *zamacueca,* a dance with African roots, was popular with the lower classes in the nineteenth century. It was the ancestor of today's more familiar *marinera.*]

6. Cañete to Pisco

1. Don Antonio Fernández de Prada, marquis of Las Torres de Orán, my host at Chincha, came to see me in London in September 1857, bringing two works by Colonel Don Juan Espinosa entitled *La herencia española de los americanos* and *Diccionario para el pueblo republicano democrático, moral, político y filosófico* which that author had requested him to deliver to me. Colonel Espinosa was a hero of Ayacucho. Don Antonio was at Morley's Hotel.
2. ["And thou shalt have a paddle upon thy weapon; and it shall be, when thou wilt ease thyself abroad, thou shalt dig therewith, and shalt turn back and cover that which cometh from thee."]

9. Ayacucho

1. [Hemming writes that the city was founded on January 9, 1539. See John Hemming, *The Conquest of the Incas,* p. 241.]
2. [This story is apocryphal. Santa Cruz's antecedents were far less mysterious. See Alfonso Crespo, *Santa Cruz: el condor indio,* pp. 17–21.]
3. [The story of the proposal is apocryphal. Narváez never served in America. Also note that the "old" lady was forty-eight or forty-nine at the time.]

10. Excursions from Ayacucho

1. [This is a reference to the famous event that occurred off the coast of Ecuador before the Spanish conquest, when Pizarro drew a line in the sand and invited his bedraggled and dispirited forces to cross it and support further exploration in search of the Inca empire.]

2. [Markham seems to have combined two royalists, Pedro de Vergara and Juan Vélez de Guevara, into one.]

11. Ayacucho to Cuzco

1. Squier gives the length of the bridge as 145 feet, height above the river 118 feet. Gibbon says the length is 324 feet, height 150 feet. [Markham seems to have taken both sets of figures from E. G. Squier, *Peru: Incidents of Travel and Exploration in the Land of the Incas*, p. 548. However, he has misquoted Squier's figure for the length: it should be 148 feet. And Lardner Gibbon actually says that the bridge was 80 yards long. See *Exploration of the Valley of the Amazon, made under direction of the Navy Department*, p. 38. Adding to the confusion are Markham's own two different figures for the height of the bridge above the river.]

12. Cuzco

1. [Lockhart lists a Miguel Estete as one of the conquistadores. However, he departed Peru in 1534, shortly after the conquest, so that it is questionable whether he left behind his name and progeny. Any child left behind would have had an Indian mother. See James Lockhart, *The Men of Cajamarca*, pp. 265–67.]

2. [Brundage argues for a later date for the construction of the Colcampata. Hemming and others note that it was the palace of the Inca Husacar (ca. 1525–1532). See Burr Cartwright Brundage, *Empire of the Inca*, pp. 147, 277; Hemming, *The Conquest of the Incas*, p. 258.]

3. [Markham's dating of the various ruins and his references to so-called monolithic and megalithic ages are now known to be incorrect. Tiahuanaco, on the shores of Lake Titicaca in present-day Bolivia, was the center of a pre-Inca civilization, while Pachacuti built Ollantaytambo and began the construction of Sacsahuaman. See Hemming, *The Conquest of the Incas*, pp. 196, 213–14.]

4. [I have been unable to locate the source of this quotation. It may be Markhams's own work.]

5. 1914: Victoria Novoa tells me that a rascally *cura* at Santa Ana sold the pictures and that they are now in Italy. [This is incorrect, as are some of Markham's assumptions about the pictures. They can presently be seen in the Archbishop's Palace in Cuzco. See Hemming's description of them in *The Conquest of the Incas*, p. 341n.]

13. The Valley of the Vilcamayo

1. [An *encomienda* was a grant to a Spanish settler of the right to extract goods and labor services from the Indians of a specified geographical area. In return, the

grantee or *encomendero* was expected to protect the assigned Indians and see to their spiritual welfare. With regard to Manco, Markham has miscounted the number of Incas: the thirteenth was Atahualpa. Manco was his half-brother, chosen by the Spaniards after Atahualpa's execution to be their puppet and a means to control the Indian population. Markham's genealogy also is open to doubt. Lockhart refers to a Pedro Ortiz as one of the conquistadores, but notes that the last reference to him was in 1534. Hemming mentions the existence of a Pedro Ortiz, a Sancho Ortiz de Orúe, and a Pedro de Orúe. He states that it was the last-named who married the Inca princess. See Lockhart, *The Men of Cajamarca*, pp. 233–34; Hemming, *The Conquest of the Incas*, pp. 611, 634.]

2. [Markham is wrong about the origins of Ollantaytambo, for we now know it was built by Pachacuti. Moreover, it was a temple as well as being a fortress. See Hemming, *The Conquest of the Incas*, pp. 213–14.]

3. [Markham published a number of accounts of the story of Apu Ollantay. See, for example, *Ollanta, an Ancient Ynca Drama* and *The Incas of Peru*, appendix D.]

4. [Markham made a drawing of the house of Señora Ampuero, noting on it, "where I first met Victoria Novoa, and thought her fair."]

15. Across the Andes from Cuzco to Arequipa

1. [It is interesting that Markham makes no comment upon this rather obvious irregularity for a priest.]

2. Vega did not turn out well and came to no good. Villegas died of fever at Lima in 1855. Dr. Berrio was afterwards well off and died in 1889.

3. Also called Nievería. Among other interesting relics, several *estolicas* have been found at Nievería. They are for hurling darts, being substitutes for bows. [Markham is incorrect about the ruins. Cajamarquilla and Nievería are proximate to one another but they are ruins of two separate civilizations, the latter being slightly later.]

Bibliographical Essay

THE UNPUBLISHED material that was used for this book, other than the manuscript itself, was located primarily in the Markham Special Collection in the Royal Geographical Society, London. Particularly useful were C. R. Markham, "Journal, Mar. 6, 1854, to Nov. 18, 1857," No. 49; C. R. Markham, "Journal, Sept. 7th, 1844, to Aug. 10, 1845," No. 2; C. R. Markham, "Private Journal kept during the voyages and journeys from Southampton to Arequipa, 1859–1860," Nos. 5, 51, 52, and 64; C. R. Markham, "Short biographical notices of old shipmates," No. 10; C. R. Markham, "Story of my service in the *Victory, Bellerophon, Sidon, Superb,* and in the *Assistance* during the Arctic Expedition of 1850–51," No. 40; "Correspondence," No. 36; D. R. Markham, "Diaries of Rev. D. R. Markham 1848–1853," No. 24. Other unpublished information was found in the Foreign Office files in the Public Record Office, London.

The only biography of Markham is by Albert H. Markham, *The Life of Sir Clements R. Markham K.C.B., F.R.S.* (London: John Murray, 1917). It is uncritical and sycophantic. A less laudatory picture of Markham in later life can be found in two volumes by Roland Huntford, *The Last Place on Earth* (London: Pan Books, 1985) and *Shackleton* (London: Hodder and Stoughton, 1985). Questions about Markham's skills as a translator were raised in Harry Bernstein and Bailey W. Diffie, "Sir Clements R. Markham as a translator," *Hispanic American Historical Review* 17 (1937): 546–57; and Bailey W. Diffie, "A Markham Contribution to the *Leyenda Negra*," *Hispanic American Historical Review* 16 (1936): 96–103.

For the historical background to Markham's visit, see Rubén Vargas Ugarte, *Historia general del Perú*, 10 vols. (Lima: Editor Carlos Milla Batres, 1966), a general work that covers both the years of Markham's visit as well as the earlier periods he mentions. See also Markham's own book, *A History of Peru* (Chicago: Charles H. Sergel and Company, 1892). For the period of the independence wars and subsequently, the most detailed work is Jorge Basadre, *Historia de la república del Perú 1822–1933*, 6th ed., 16 vols. (Lima: Editorial Universitaria, 1969–1970). A survey in English with chapters on the early nineteenth century is Fredrick B. Pike, *The Modern History of Peru* (London: Weidenfeld and Nicolson, 1967).

For the history of the Incas and the conquest of Peru, Markham lists as the sources he consulted or was advised to read: José de Acosta, *Historia natural y moral de las Indias, en que se tratan las cosas notables del cielo, elementos, metales, plantas y animales de ellas; y los ritos, ceremonias, leyes, gobierno y guerras de los Indios*, 6th ed. (Madrid: P. Aznar, 1792); Pedro de Cieza de León, *La crónica del Perú* (Anvers: Martín Nucio, 1554); Diego Fernández, *Primera y segunda parte de la historia del Perú* (Sevilla: Impreso en casa de H. Diaz, 1571); Garcilaso de la Vega, el Inca, *The Royal Commentaries of Peru, in two parts*, trans. Sir Paul Rycaut (London: Printed by M. Flesher, 1688); Francisco López de Gómara, *La historia general de las Indias y Nuevo Mundo*, 2 vols. (Zaragoza: Pedro Bermuz, 1554); Antonio de Herrera y Tordesillas, *Historia general de los hechos de los castellanos en las islas i tierra firme del mar oceano*, 4 vols. (Madrid: Imprenta Real, 1601–1615); Fernando Montesinos, *Memorias antiguas historiales y políticas del Perú* (Madrid: Impr. de M. Ginesta, 1882); Pedro Pizarro, *Relación del descubrimiento y conquista de los reinos del Perú, y del gobierno y órden que los naturales tenian, y tesoros que en ella se hallaron* (Madrid: n.p., 1844); Juan Polo de Ondegardo, *Informaciones acerca de la religión y gobierno de los Incas* (n.p., 1571); William Hickling Prescott, *History of the Conquest of Peru, with a preliminary view of the Civilization of the Incas*, 2 vols. (London: Richard Bentley, 1847); Mariano Eduardo de Rivero y Ustáriz and Juan Diego von Tschudi, *Antigüedades Peruanas* (Vienna: Imp. Imperial de la Corte y del Estado, 1851); Justo Sahuaraura, *Recuerdos de la monarquía peruana; o, bosquejo de la historia de los incas* (Paris: De Rosa, Bouret y Cia., 1850); Agustín de Zarate, *Historia del descubrimiento y conquista de las provincias del Perú* (Sevilla: Alonso Escriuano, 1577).

To check Markham's historical and archeological details for the Inca period and the Spanish conquest, I consulted Louis Baudin, *A Socialist Empire: The Incas of Peru*, trans. Katherine Woods, ed. Arthur Goddard (Princeton: D. Van Nostrand Company, 1961); Burr Cartwright Brundage, *Empire of the Inca* (Norman: University of Oklahoma Press, 1963) and *Lords of Cuzco: A History and Description of the Inca People in Their Final Days* (Norman: University of Oklahoma Press, 1967); Cesar García Rosell, *Diccionario arqueológico del Perú* (Lima: n.p., n.d.); Garcilaso de la Vega, *The Royal Commentaries of the Incas and General History of Peru*, trans. Harold Livermore, 2 vols. (Austin: University of Texas Press, 1966); John Hemming, *The Conquest of the Incas* (London:

Macmillan, 1970); John Hemming and Edward Ranney, *Monuments of the Incas* (Boston: Little, Brown and Company, 1982); James Lockhart, *The Men of Cajamarca: A Social and Biographical Study of the First Conquerors of Peru* (Austin: University of Texas Press, 1972); J. Alden Mason, *The Ancient Civilizations of Peru* (Harmondsworth: Penguin Books, 1969). See also Markham's own works, *The Incas of Peru* (London: Smith, Elder, and Company, 1910) and *Ollanta, an Ancient Ynca Drama* (London: Trübner and Company, 1871).

Details of Peru's colonial history have been checked against Nicholas P. Cushner, *Lords of the Land: Sugar, Wine and Jesuit Estates of Coastal Peru, 1600–1767* (Albany: State University of New York Press, 1980); John R. Fisher, *Government and Society in Colonial Peru: The Intendant System 1784–1814* (London: Athlone Press, 1970); Lillian Estelle Fisher, *The Last Inca Revolt 1780–1783* (Norman: University of Oklahoma Press, 1966); James Lockhart, *Spanish Peru 1532–1560: A Colonial Society* (Madison: University of Wisconsin Press, 1968).

For the late colonial and independence periods, Markham used John Miller, *Memoirs of General Miller, in the Service of the Republic of Peru*, 2 vols. (London: Longman, Rees, Orme, Brown and Green, 1828); William Robertson, *The History of America*, 2 vols. (London: W. Strahan, 1777); Joseph Skinner, *The Present State of Peru: Comprising its geography, topography, natural history, mineralogy, commerce, the customs and manners of its inhabitants, the state of literature, philosophy, and the arts, the modern travels of the missionaries in the heretofore unexplored mountainous territories, &c. &c. The whole drawn from original and authentic documents, chiefly written and comp. in the Peruvian capital; and embellished by twenty engravings of costumes, &c.* (London: R. Phillips, 1805); Antonio de Ulloa and Jorge Juan y Santacilia, *Noticias secretas de América, sobre el estado naval, militar, y político de los reynos del Perú y provincias de Quito, costas de Nueva Granada y Chile: gobierno y regimen particular de los pueblos de Indios: cruel opresión y extorsiones de sus corregidores y curas; abusos escandalosos introducidos entre estos habitantes por los misioneros; causas de su origen y motivos de su continuación por el espacio de tres siglos* (London: R. Taylor, 1826).

A modern work on the independence period in Peru is Timothy E. Anna, *The Fall of the Royal Government in Peru* (Lincoln: University of Nebraska Press, 1979). Two chapters in John Lynch, *The Spanish American Revolutions 1808–1826* (London: Weidenfeld and Nicolson, 1973) deal with events in Peru.

Markham consulted the following travel accounts to learn more about the situation in Peru in the early nineteenth century: Robert Proctor, *Narrative of a Journey across the Cordillera of the Andes, and of a Residence in Lima, and other Parts of Peru, in the Years 1823 and 1824* (London: Archibald Constable and Company, 1825); Peter Campbell Scarlett, *South America and the Pacific: Comprising a Journey across the Pampas and the Andes, from Buenos Ayres to Valparaiso, Lima, and Panama; with Remarks upon the Isthmus,* 2 vols. (London: Henry Colburn, Publisher, 1838); Archibald Smith, *Peru As It Is: A Residence in Lima, and other parts of the Peruvian Republic, Comprising an Account of the Social and Physical Features of that Country,* 2 vols. (Lima: Richard Bentley, 1839); William Bennet Stevenson, *A Historical and Descriptive Narrative of Twenty Years' Residence in South America containing travels in Arauco, Chile, Peru, and Colombia; with an account of the revolution, its rise, progress, and results* (London: Hurst, Robinson and Company, 1825); Johann Jacob von Tschudi, *Travels in Peru, during the Years 1838–1842, on the coast, in the sierra, across the cordilleras and the Andes, into the primeval forests,* trans. Thomasina Ross (London: David Bogue, 1847). Other travel accounts to which he refers are Lardner Gibbon, *Exploration of the Valley of the Amazon, made under direction of the Navy Department* (Washington, D.C.: A. O. P. Nicholson, Public Printer, 1854); E. George Squier, *Peru: Incidents of Travel and Exploration in the Land of the Incas* (New York: Harper and Brothers, Publishers, 1877); Pedro Félix Vicuña, *Ocho meses de destierro o cartas sobre el Perú* (Valparaíso: Librería del Mercurio, 1847). To this list should be added Markham's own *Cuzco: A Journey to the Ancient Capital of Peru; with an account of the history, language, literature, and antiquities of the Incas. And Lima. A Visit to the Capital and Provinces of Modern Peru; with a sketch of the viceregal government, history of the republic, and a review of the literature and society of Peru* (London: Chapman and Hall, 1856). It was republished in 1973 by the Kraus Reprint Company of Millwood, N.Y. Markham's account of his final trip to Peru in 1860 can be found in *Travels in Peru and India while superintending the collection of chinchona plants and seeds in South America, and their introduction into India* (London: John Murray, 1862). Another travel account for the early nineteenth century that is worth reading and is now available in English is Flora Tristán, *Peregrinations of a Pariah 1833–1834,* trans. and ed. Jean Hawkes (London: Virago Press, 1986).

For particular developments in Peru during the period of Markham's visit, see W. M. Mathew, *The House of Gibbs and the Peruvian Guano Monopoly* (London: Royal Historical Society, 1981), which examines the guano industry; and Watt Stewart, *Chinese Bondage in Peru. A History of the Chinese Coolie in Peru, 1849–1874* (Durham: Duke University Press, 1951), which provides details of the Chinese coolie trade.

Information on historical figures Markham mentions can be found in Manuel de Mendiburu, *Diccionario histórico-biográfico del Perú,* 8 vols. (Lima: Imp. de J. F. Solis, 1874–1890); Evaristo San Cristóbal, *Apendice al diccionario histórico-biográfico del Perú,* 4 vols. (Lima: Librería e imprenta Gil, 1935). The family background of the Bolivian independence hero Andrés de Santa Cruz can be found in Alfonso Crespo, *Santa Cruz: el condor indio* (Mexico City: Fondo de Cultura Económica, 1944). Placenames were checked against those listed in Mariano Felipe Paz Soldán, *Atlas geográfico de la república del Perú* (Paris: Librería de F. Brachet, 1869) and *Diccionario geográfico estadístico del Perú* (Lima: Imprenta del Estado, 1877). The latter volume was immensely valuable in this regard. Markham compared some of the Peruvian Spanish terms he heard with entries in Juan de Arona [Pedro Paz Soldán y Unanue], *Diccionario de peruanismos, ensayo filológico* (Lima: Imp. de J. F. Solis, 1883), adding a few that Arona listed. I used Marcos A. Morínigo, *Diccionario manual de americanismos* (Buenos Aires: Muchnik Editores, 1966) to try to check Markham's accuracy. For works on the Quechua language, Markham mentions P. Diego Gonzales Holguín, *Gramática y arte nueva de la lengua general de todo el Perú, llamada lengua Quichua o lengua del Inca* (n.p., 1842); and Diego de Torres Rubio, *Arte de la lengua quichua* (Lima: Francisco Lasso, 1619). I have checked his Quechua spellings against those in Max Espinoza Galarza, *Toponimia quechua del Perú* (Lima: COSESA, 1973); and Jorge A. Lira, *Diccionario Kkechuwa— Español* (Tucumán: Universidad Nacional de Tucumán, 1944). Further information on the flora Markham encountered can be found in George Usher, *A Dictionary of Plants Used by Man* (London: Constable, 1974).

I also consulted numerous dictionaries, naval lists, civil service lists, and encyclopedias to try to locate Markham's sources and to check his spellings, his terms, and his historical details. The most useful of these was Alberto Tauro, ed., *Diccionario enciclopédico del Perú,* 4 vols. (Lima: Editorial Mejía Baca, 1966). Despite my efforts, however, I was not always successful in my search.

Index

Abancay, 81–82
Abusive language, 41–42
Aliaga, Juan, 10, 20, 43
Almagro, Diego de (father), xii, 26, 39, 74, 82, 94
Almagro, Diego de (son), 74–76, 94
Andahuaylas, 79–80
Antony Gibbs and Sons, xiii, 7, 40, 12̇
Apurímac bridge, 83, 136
Arequipa, 122–123
Artajona, Josefa Ochoa y Manrique de, 101, 104, 105, 108
Asia, 27–28
Astete de Bennet, Josefa, 89, 90, 95, 97–98, 100, 117, 124
Atahualpa, xii, 10, 137
Ayacucho, 59–68, 70, 71, 74
Ayacucho, battle of, xii, 60, 70–74, 94, 123
Ayavi, 56–57
Ayavirini, 121

Barreda, Felipe, 7, 9, 10, 40, 128
Basadre, Modesto, 10–11, 13, 89
Bolívar, Simón, xii, 63, 94
Buenamuerte order, 30, 33, 34, 35
Buenavista estate, 20
Bujama estate, 26
Bullfight, 12

Cajamarquilla, 125, 137
Callao, ix, x, 6, 124
Calmet, Francisco, 39, 43, 45

Cañete Valley, 28–37, 38
Canopa, 33, 90, 102
Canseco, Jesusa, 64, 65, 129
Carhuacarhua estate, 81
Carpio, Agustín, 54–60
Casa Blanca estate, 30, 33
Castilla, Gen. Ramón, xiii, 9, 10, 12, 73, 87, 127–128
Caucato estate, 42
Cerro Blanco mine, 50–51
Chaclacayo, 16, 17
Chasquihuasi estate, 117
Chavalina estate, 53–54
Chilca, 24–26
Chincha Islands, 39–41
Chinchero, 105–106
Chinese, xiv, 6, 16, 23, 31, 33, 39
Chorrillos, 17, 18, 20, 24, 125, 129
Chumpitasy, José, 25
Chunchos, 112–113
Chupas, battle of, 74–76
Cinchona, xiv, 108, 111, 113, 114
Cintura, José, 46–47, 52
Cocachacra, 17
Cochrane, Thomas, 44, 59
Cock fight, 34, 35
Codecido family, 7, 10
Colcampata, 89–91, 95, 136
Colley Head Society, 13, 134
Collingwood, H. M. S., x, xi, xii, 6, 8, 17, 27, 87, 124
Colón, 3
Condorcanqui, José Gabriel. See

Túpac Amaru II
Cosñipata estate, 111, 113
Cotes, Manuel M., 7, 8, 12, 13, 85, 96, 97, 134
Cotton, xiii, 46, 47, 49, 50, 52
Cruces, 4
Curahuasi, 82–83
Curamba, 81
Cuzco, ix, x, 11, 76, 85–99, 115–117

Díaz, Gaspar, 12
Dickens, Charles, 134

Earthquake, 10, 20–21
Echenique, Gen. José Rufino, 8–9, 87, 127–128, 134
Elguera, Pablo, 20–21
Elías, Domingo, 13, 39, 40, 41, 42–43, 46, 47, 49, 52
English residents, 7–8, 20, 30, 33, 41, 123, 124

Fernández, Dr. Martín, 26
Frías, Manuel, 45, 52

Garcilaso de la Vega, el Inca, xvii, 1, 27, 87, 91, 95, 111
Gomes estate, 36–37
Gorgona, 3–4
Guano, xiii, 6, 39–41, 43
Guarda, Gen. Manuel de la, 13, 85, 87–88, 98, 107–108, 115, 117, 127–128

Hartrick, 15–17
Hatun-sulla, 59
Herbay, 37–38, 51
Hermosa, José María, 79–80
Herrera, Manuela, 48
Huaca, 11, 21, 30, 33, 39, 48
Huaca estate, 28–36
Huaccac-pata, 82
Huamanga. *See* Ayacucho
Huancarama, 81
Huanta, 69–70
Huatanay River, 11, 87, 89, 91,

96–97, 100

Ica, 45–46, 52–53
Incas, ix, xii, xiv, 8–9, 10–11, 12, 38, 48, 71, 81, 84, 87, 93, 97, 101, 102, 117, 118, 134, 136, 137; ruins, 16, 37–38, 49, 51–52, 84, 88, 89–92, 94–97, 101–106, 109, 114, 117, 136
Independence wars, xii, xiii, 11–12, 44, 70, 123. *See also* Ayacucho, battle of
Indians, xiv, 10–11, 17, 21, 25, 43–45, 54, 58, 65–68, 70, 76, 79, 81, 83, 89, 91, 97, 98, 100, 104, 106, 107, 109, 111, 114, 117, 118, 120. *See also* Chunchos; Incas; Iquichanos
Iquichanos, 70

Jesuits, 42, 43, 49, 54, 88, 93, 94
Justiniani, Dr. Pablo Policarpo, 106–107

Lacras. *See* Santa Isabel de Lacras estate
La Cueva de San Luis, 58
Ladd, Isaac, 46, 47, 49
La Hoya estate, 43, 44
La Máquina estate, 52
La Merced church, Cuzco, 76–89, 93–94
Langui, 119
La Puerta, José, 108, 116, 118, 121, 122, 123–124
Larán estate, 38–39
Lares, 106–107
Lásquez, Mariano, 24
Lima, 6, 7–14, 17, 22–23, 124–125
Limatambo, 84, 90
Lobos Afuera Island, 6
Lomitas, 47
Los Frayles, 121, 130
Lurín, 24

Madre de Dios River, 112, 113
Mala, 26

Maras, 100–101, 105
Markham, Rev. David F., x, xi–xii, 99, 125
Martínez, José Blas Santos, 45, 52–53
Mataratones. *See* San Juan de Arona estate
Mellena, José, 23–26, 28
Military, xiii, 6, 73, 123
Mining, xiii, 9, 15, 43, 50–51, 52, 57, 134
Miranda y Vengoa, Francisco, 88
Mollepata, 83–84
Montalván estate, 30, 34
Montaña, 54, 98, 110–114
Morin's Hotel, 6, 22, 124
Mosol, Col. Antonio, 63, 70, 73, 129

Narváez, Ramón María, 62, 73, 135
Nazarenes church, Cuzco, 94
Nazca, 49–52
Negroes, 17, 18, 20–21, 23, 24, 27, 30, 31, 32, 35, 36, 37, 39, 51. *See also* Slaves
New York, 3
Nievería, 137
Novoa, Manuel, 108, 116, 117, 118, 120, 131
Novoa, Victoria, xv, 108, 116–124, 130–132, 136, 137

Ochoa, Dr. Julián, 88, 89, 90, 95, 98, 116–117
Ocoruro, 120
Ocros, 78
Ocucaje estate, 46, 47
Ollantaytambo, 91, 101–105, 108, 109, 136, 137
Osma, Mariano de, 13, 29–30, 33–36

Pachacámac, 17–18, 20, 24
Pachacutec (Pachacuti) Inca, 87, 90, 91, 96, 136, 137
Palpa, 52
Panama (city), 4–5
Panama, Isthmus of, 3–4

Paucartambo, 110–111, 114
Paz Soldán, Pedro, 30, 31, 34, 135
Paz Soldán y Unanue, Pedro, 135
Pepperell, 2–3
Perry, William, 5
Pezet, Gen. Juan Antonio, 73, 122–123
Pisac, 109
Pisco, 39, 42–43
Pizarro, Francisco, xii, 26, 39, 62, 74, 75, 136
Portland, H. M. S., 124–125
Prada, Antonio Fernández de, 38, 39, 135
Prescott, Amory, 2, 3
Prescott, William Hickling, xi, xii, 1–2, 84
Priests, 10–11, 26, 31, 33, 34, 35, 53, 67, 80, 84, 88, 100–101, 105, 112–113, 114. *See also* Justiniani, Dr. Pablo Policarpo; Ochoa, Dr. Julián; Revello, Dr. Bovo de; Taforo, Dr. Francisco de Paula; Tapia y Guaycochea, Dr. José Manuel
Pueblo Viejo de Cañete, 34–35
Pumacahua, Mateo García, 11, 89, 90, 134

Quebrada estate, 28, 30, 33, 34, 35
Quechua, xi, xvi, 12, 41, 56, 62, 63, 65–66, 67, 98, 105, 106, 107, 114, 119, 120, 123
Quintana, Juan de Dios, 45, 53–54

Reid, W., 30, 33, 34
Religious celebrations, 25, 35, 82–83, 85, 88, 97, 118
Religious orders, 10–11, 42, 49, 64–65, 94, 95, 96, 97, 100, 107. *See also* Buenamuerte order; Jesuits
Revello, Dr. Bovo de, 111, 112–114, 115
Robbers, xiii, 15, 17, 18, 20, 24
Rocca Inca, 94, 95

Sacsahuaman, 86, 87, 90–93, 136
San Borja college, 94
San Cristóbal church, Cuzco, 90
San Javier estate, 49, 52
San Juan de Arona estate, 30, 31–32, 34, 135
San Miguel estate, 112, 113
San Pedro estate, 20
Santa Ana, 47, 48
Santa Ana church, Cuzco, 97, 136
Santa Cruz, Gen. Andrés de, 34, 62, 63, 87, 135
Santa Isabel de Lacras estate, 49
Santo Domingo church, Cuzco, 94, 95–96
Saya y manto, 7, 12, 134
Slaves, ix, xiv, 15, 18, 31, 49, 53, 54. *See also* Negroes
Sugar, xiii, 18, 20, 30–33, 38, 42, 80, 81, 82, 84
Superb, H. M. S., x, 5, 134

Taforo, Dr. Francisco de Paula, xv, 68, 79–85, 98, 108, 115, 116–123, 128, 129–130
Tambillo, 55, 56
Tapia y Guaycochea, Dr. José Manuel, 114
Tartana estate, 65

Tello y Cabrera, Manuel, 60, 62–65, 67, 68, 70, 74, 128–129; family, 62–65, 67–68, 74, 76, 78, 128–129
Temple of the Sun. *See* Santo Domingo church, Cuzco
Terracing, 55, 84, 101, 102, 104, 105, 109
Tijero, José Mariano, 52
Tirado, Manuel, 8, 9
Torre Tagle palace, 11
Torrico, Gen. Crisóstomo, 6, 8, 13, 22, 28, 73, 85, 135
Trigoso, Basilio, 50–52
Túpac Amaru II, xi, 94, 106, 118, 119

Ugalde, Manuel, 98, 112
Urubamba, 105, 106, 107, 108

Vilcamayo Valley, 98, 100–109, 117
Villacuri estate, 44–45
Villa estate, 18, 20
Vineyards, 39, 42–43, 49, 50, 52, 53–54

Yanaoca, 118–119
Yauca, 53
Yucay, 101, 105